History of England

A Captivating Guide to English History,
Starting from Antiquity through the Rule of
the Anglo-Saxons, Vikings, Normans, and
Tudors to the End of World War 2

Free Bonus from Captivating History
(Available for a Limited time)

Hi History Lovers!

Now you have a chance to join our exclusive history list so you can get your first history ebook for free as well as discounts and a potential to get more history books for free! Simply visit the link below to join.

Captivatinghistory.com/ebook

Also, make sure to follow us on Facebook, Twitter and Youtube by searching for Captivating History.

Contents

Introduction

There are few places that entice the imagination quite like England. Just a little island off the western coast of continental Europe, it boasts a rich history that stretches all the way back to the first modern humans. Since then, entire societies have risen and fallen as people learned to make flint and bone tools, bury their dead, and fortify their cities against foreign raiders. From the fearsome Celtic warriors of prehistory to the clever inventors and statesmen of the modern era, England's story is one bursting with magnificent castles, complex kings and queens, rebellious peasants, and horrifying plagues.

Throughout history, more people have called England home than perhaps most of us have ever realized.

Chapter One – The People of Prehistory

Around 900,000 years ago, the earliest known human beings appeared in the British Isles.[1] Nearly a million years before written records began, these lands underwent massive changes in climate, culture, government, engineering, and geology. The discovery of 900,000-year-old flint tools throughout modern Britain reveals a small part of the lives of a semi-nomadic early species of human that actually did not have to travel by boat to reach Britain but only had to walk across the land bridge from northern mainland Europe.

Anthropologists hypothesize that these early humans spent time in Britain mostly during the warmer summer months. There is little evidence of permanent settlements in this area until about 500,000 years ago; after this time, several species of proto-humans appear to have frequented the landscape. Some of these visitors and potential residents were Neanderthals. Little of significance has been found of these early peoples, but starting about 30,000 years ago, the archaeological record shows a clear increase in population and cultural evolution. By that period, modern humans had emerged.

---

[1] "Prehistory." *English Heritage.* Web.

They hunted mostly wild horses and red deer, subsisting on hunting and gathering methods through the Ice Age.

As the Ice Age came to a gradual close, the ground warmed slowly, and forests began to stretch across the landscape. More people settled in the area, creating an ancient culture whose components researchers can only guess at. Eventually, they began to leave more compelling clues as to their identities. On the border of Nottinghamshire and Derbyshire sits Creswell Crags, an area with many cave formations. In the rock known as the Church Hole at Nottinghamshire, engravings were discovered on the cave walls, dating from about 13,000 years ago.[2] Birds, buffalo, deer, and bears are shown in the engravings, which is the earliest form of cave art found in Britain.

At the end of the Ice Age, around 6500 BCE, rising sea levels finally cut off the British peninsula from the rest of Europe, making the islands that we recognize today.[3] About 2,000 years later, farming technology began to revolutionize food production among the people of Britain.[4] The objects these first farmers and their successors left behind include stone ax heads, querns for grinding flour, and ard plows. Farming had already been in use in Greece, the Mediterranean, and the Middle East for about 5,000 years at this point, and archeologists posit that a large and sudden influx of immigrants from mainland Europe may explain the transition in Britain. Others suggest that intermingling between eastern and western cultures brought in the new methods over a longer period of time. People who brought the methods to the island had to go by boat from continental Europe to England, which would not have been an easy task.

---

[2] "Sistine Chapel of the Ice Age." *BBC News*. Web. 2004.

[3] "An Introduction to Prehistoric England (Before AD 43)." *English Heritage*. Web.

[4] Ibid.

While England's early residents mostly cultivated barley and wheat, people were still dependent on the wild for other types of food. They still moved around from region to region rather than settling in one location, suggesting that hunting went hand in hand with growing crops; as time went on, however, villages and urban centers began to appear on the landscape.

Between around 3500 and 3300 BCE, farming communities began to focus on more fertile regions, including eastern Scotland, Anglesey, the Upper Thames, Wessex, Suffolk, Yorkshire, and the river valleys of Wash, which are the most productive in terms of soil and agricultural output.[5] Clusters of villages appeared in the most fertile areas of Britain throughout the Neolithic Period, which is indicative of a more settled way of life and higher importance placed on farmed foods. These settlement areas would persist and rise in population slowly, meaning that these would remain principal regions of the country in far future eras.

The homes built by Neolithic Britons were generally rectangular and constructed from wood. With such masses of forested areas, wood was a plentiful and valuable commodity. In cutting down trees to make more agricultural space, people simultaneously were able to use that wood to construct buildings and keep home fires burning. The foundations of such structures, though rare and usually only discovered nearby larger stone Neolithic monuments, are an important part of the archaeological record.

Indeed, the most formative feature of Britain's Neolithic Age—at least from what we can still see—are the burial edifices. Massive mounds, like Silbury Hill in Wiltshire or the chambered tomb at Newgrange in Ireland, were scattered heavily across the ancient land in a dazzling show of cultural evolution. Anthropologists believe this signified a newfound veneration of one's ancestors, family, and perhaps powerful social leaders. The weapons, stone henges, wood

---

[5] Pearson, Mike Parker. *Bronze Age Britain (Revised Edition)*. 2005.

henges, hill forts, and burial sites of these ancient peoples can still be found by archaeologists today. Evidence of their urban centers includes civic monuments such as Stonehenge or the Windmill Hill enclosure, both of which were built in Wiltshire around the end of the Neolithic Revolution. Other monuments built by these Bronze Age societies included sepulchers with impressive barrows mounded over the burial chamber of important dead citizens.

These burial rituals evolved over the next few millennia, becoming vast henges, massive stone works, and eventually the large Iron Age hillforts of the Celts. As the Britons flourished, however, their land and resources became a source of jealousy for other European leaders. The powerful Roman ruler, Julius Caesar, sent a military outpost to Britain expecting to conquer it outright; his forces failed in this mission, however. It was not until 43 CE that the ancient peoples of Britain faced their most confusing and fearsome foe: Roman Emperor Claudius.[6]

---

[6] Faulker, Dr. Neil. "Overview: Roman Britain, 43 - 410 AD." *BBC History.* Web. 2011.

Chapter Two – The Roman Conquest

The decision to send the famed Roman army all the way into Britain was a strange political move for the most powerful empire in Europe. The Roman Republic—followed by the Roman Empire— had already claimed the lands surrounding the Mediterranean Sea, those of the Germanic tribes and the Gauls, and even cities as far east as Mesopotamia. There was little economic reason to continue pushing Roman forces farther west, except that the new emperor, Claudius, needed an exciting project to make him more likable.

Claudius inherited the emperorship after his brother, the infamously "mad" Emperor Caligula, was assassinated in 41 CE.[7] The Roman Senate was not in favor of Claudius as a ruler, particularly given his relationship to the old emperor. Knowing this, Claudius needed a quick political solution to protect his throne, and he chose to placate the masses with some old-fashioned empire-building. To the Romans of his day, Britain was a thing of fantasy and wonder; it was at the farthest reaches of the known world, and not even the great Julius Caesar had been able to take it by force. It was a place of the

---

[7] Ibid.

marsh and wood, populated by fierce blue-painted warriors, and it dominated the popular imagination. To propose a campaign in Britain was a very clever and successful move on the part of the unpopular Emperor Claudius, though he was not around very long to enjoy the fruits of his campaign. Claudius died soon after his armies arrived on the distant island, in 54 CE, probably by poisoning from his wife or one of the Roman senators.[8]

The invasion brought together an army of 40,000 professional soldiers.[9] Half were civilian legionaries, and half were auxiliaries who were recruited or enslaved from Rome's distant provinces. The man charged with leading the army into this foreign territory and overcoming the native Britons was Aulus Plautius. Dutifully, Plautius led his men to the island and likely landed in the southeast, according to archaeological data. Once situated, the Romans attacked and subdued the local Catuvellauni tribe. Moving onward, the Romans encountered many communities of diverse Celts, but it was Queen Boudicca of the Celtic Iceni tribe who put up the most famous fight against them.

Boudicca was the wife to King Prasutagus of the Iceni, and both ruled over a tribe located approximately in what is today's Norfolk. Contemporaries identified Boudica as a tall queen, with long red hair and a rough voice. She is said to have worn a thick, golden ring around her neck. When the encamped Romans were busy commandeering a small settlement on the River Thames, Boudicca was plotting to destroy the powerful enemy that had moved onto her ancestral lands. Her desire for vengeance was made much greater by the fact that the Romans had not only refused to respect her daughters' right to rule Iceni upon the death of King Prasutagus in 59 CE but that the soldiers had also tortured the women as well.

---

[8] "Claudius (10 BC - 54 AD)." *BBC History*. Web.

[9] "Five things we get wrong about the Roman conquest of Britain." *BBC*. Web.

Boudicca gathered her own warriors and struck up an alliance with other native Britons in order to lay siege to the Roman encampments. They started in Camulodunum, where modern Colchester stands, and razed it to the ground. Catus Decianus, the Roman in command of the outpost, was forced to flee outright, and afterward, the tribespeople besieged the Temple of Claudius for two days. A faction of the Roman army was instructed to finish off the rebels, but they were forced to retreat.

There is archaeological evidence that corroborates the story of Boudicca's violent foray through Roman-occupied lands in Britain, particularly in south London. There, pottery and coins have been found at various depths in the soil, providing a clear timeline for researchers. A road, constructed in about 50 CE and lined by houses and shops, has been discovered among the items.[10] All of these were burned to the ground soon after having been built—right around the time Boudicca is reported to have killed as many as 70,000 Romans and razed the fledgling community of Londinium, a city that would one day become London.[11] The encounter has been dubbed the "Battle of Watling Street" due to the location of the archaeological findings. A matching layer of scorch marks has been found on the north bank of London as well.

During Boudicca's campaign, the Iceni tribespeople performed sacrifices to their goddess Andraste, the Celtic goddess of revenge. The Roman historian Cassius Dio wrote of the scene in which Boudicca addressed her warriors:

> 'Let us, therefore, go against (the romans), trusting boldly to good fortune. Let us show them that they are hares and foxes trying to rule over dogs and wolves.' when she (boudicca) had finished speaking, she employed a species of divination, letting a hare escape from the fold of her dress; and since it ran on what they considered the auspicious side, the whole multitude shouted with pleasure, and boudicca, raising her hand toward heaven, said: 'i thank you, andraste, and call

---

[10] Muir, Hazel. "Boudicca rampaged through the streets of south London." *New Scientist.* Web. 1995.

[11] Ibid.

upon you as woman speaking to woman…i beg you for victory and preservation of liberty.'[12]

The iceni lost this final battle against the romans, and 80,000 men and women, including queen boudicca, perished.[13] the records concerning the queen's death are conflicting. Cassius dio states that she died of illness during the course of the rebellion, while another roman historian, tacitus, wrote that she poisoned herself rather than succumb to the romans' swords.[14]

---

[12] Dio Cassius, as quoted by *English Monarchs.* "Boudicca, Queen of the Iceni." Web.

[13] Ibid.

[14] Ibid.

Chapter Three – Britannia

The Battle of Watling Street between Boudicca and the Romans was the last major threat to Roman authority in the lowlands of what they called Britannia. The Roman governor, Gaius Suetonius Paulinus, the very same man who had orchestrated the new wave of conquest, did not only fight against Boudicca but also demolished the Druid fortress in Anglesey. Though the fortress and other small communities were considered to be a threat to Roman occupation, Paulinus' continued violence against the native groups of Britain began to raise moral concerns. Using a brutal and violent strategy, the governor may have been able to force the subjugation of Boudicca's people, but his excessive force—unusual even for a Roman warrior—led to his removal from the governorship. He was replaced by Publius Petronius Turpilianus in 61 CE, and Rome attempted to move forward in a more diplomatic way with the Britons from that point onward.

With diplomacy gaining ground, Roman culture gradually seeped into the landscape of the Britons. Ravaged communities were rebuilt, and in very little time, Londinium was reestablished with a basilica, a forum, a governor's mansion, and a sturdy bridge across the River

Thames. Soon, the previously small and overlooked town became Roman Britain's administrative center. Although progress was slow, a succession of Roman emperors continued investing in the realm's expansion for economic reasons. Though Julius Caesar had famously rejected the island as being of no importance, in reality, Britannia possessed a wealth of mineral resources. There was copper, iron, and gold to be mined in plenty, as well as trained hunting dogs and other valuable animals.

The Roman conquerors pressed ahead, engaging some natives in war and befriending others, all while its soldiers worked hard to develop a Roman-style infrastructure. They built roads and cities with forums at their centers, and they also developed a mining industry. There were many resources already in Britannia that helped ease the Romans' effort; however, the new society also imported huge amounts of its own traditional staples, including rice, cattle, and foreign slaves. Rich in food and labor, Rome made significant inroads to Britannia, quite literally, in fact. A network of roads was constructed that connected large outposts, including the communities of Londinium and Eboracum, the latter of which is now known as York. With the roads and cities thriving, traders came to ply their goods and services, and the population of Romans residing in Britannia increased quickly.

Military commander Gnaeus Julius Agricola was appointed as the governor of Britannia between 77 and 83 CE, having already served there during his youth as a military tribune under Governor Paulinus. Agricola wrote about the time he had spent in Britannia and Germany during his early days with the Roman army, and he told contemporaries that though he was excited to take part in the venture, he was careful never to let his guard down. He wrote, "Neither before nor since has Britain ever been in a more uneasy or dangerous state. Veterans were butchered, colonies burned to the ground, armies isolated. We had to fight for life before we could think of victory."[15]

Agricola led his fellow Romans in a series of battles with the Britons, who refused to make concessions to him, and he ultimately managed to subdue North Wales and part of Scotland. He considered the prospect of crossing the Irish Sea to take the smaller Irish island and guessed that it could be conquered with just a single Roman legion. This plan never came to fruition, however, since some of Agricola's legions were called back by Emperor Domitian to help defend Rome against an enemy on mainland Europe. The loss of these soldiers set Agricola back in Scotland as well, but his gains were not completely lost. Largely because of Governor Agricola's campaigns in the west and north of Britannia, more native Britons than ever before were personally exposed to Roman culture. Urbanization flourished as people moved to cities to experience the forums, baths, and theaters and to sample the imported foods, machines, and textiles from the massive Roman Empire.

Agricola was the first governor of Britannia to embark on a campaign of Romanization, a policy in which he meant to change the culture of the Britons into that of the Romans. He fought when and where he needed to in order to protect what he and his people had built, but his overarching policy was that of wiping out the native cultures and replacing it with his own. Like many Romans, Agricola believed that the Roman Empire was the greatest in the world, not only because of its size and power but also because of its educational system, artisans, social structure, and beliefs. At Agricola's behest, the Romans began teaching the Britons how to use Latin.

A few decades after Agricola's governorship ended, the ashes of Londinium had been completely covered over and expanded with new homes, workshops, and public monuments. This time, the village was much larger and was characterized by big stone

---

[15] Quoted by Wasson, Donald L. "Roman Britain." *Ancient History Encyclopedia.* Web. 30 January 2017.

foundations that have been dated to earlier than 120 CE.[16] Archaeologists believe that this immense and long-winded rebuilding project culminated just in time to have Londinium looking powerful and grand for Emperor Hadrian's arrival. It was during this period that the humble Londinium earned the investments necessary to propel it to even greater importance within Britannia. All across Britain, the seeds of Emperor Claudius' vision had begun to take root.

Emperor Hadrian visited Britannia in about 120 CE, and though it would still be years before the Roman territory reached completely into Scotland, he commissioned a massive wall in the northern edge of the realm.[17] Hadrian's Wall, which began construction in 122, stretched 117 kilometers in length (73 miles) and required 15,000 soldiers to man it.[18] Realizing that he could not properly begin expansion northward until the Romans and the Scots had reached a certain level of diplomacy, Hadrian meant for the wall to act as a surveillance point between the two people. Of course, it could also easily function as a way to keep out raiders and armies from the northern lands.

Over the next decade, Rome fortified Britannia extensively with forts and other walls, which were necessary to protect the Roman Britons from attacks by Celts and Picts on all sides. In the 3rd century CE, there were also invasions by people of the Germanic tribes, as well as insurrections from two Roman Britons. First Carausius, then Allectus, headed rebellions that led to a short-lived independence from Rome. By that time, the Roman Empire had become too cumbersome to remain politically stable and had split into a Western and Eastern empire. The Western Emperor Constantius I fought back against the rogue kingdom of Britannia and wrested it back into his

---

[16] Ibid.

[17] Ibid.

[18] Ibid.

control in 296 CE.[19] The victorious emperor was already well known and loved in Britannia, as he had served there as a military tribune many years earlier; this reputation helped him get the realm back in check. The Britons loyal to Rome greatly appreciated having them back in the empire, as they, too, largely considered the Romans to have the most learned and worthy of all cultures on Earth. In Londinium, Emperor Constantius I was given the title "The Restorer of the Eternal Light."

[19] Ibid.

Chapter Four – The Dark Ages

Just a century after Emperor Constantius restored Britannia to its light, Emperor Honorius found himself with no choice but to extinguish the light of Rome there forever. It is largely due to this ancient metaphor that Rome and its protectors were like the "light" and that everyone else lived in the darkness that we have the unofficial moniker for this period of history in England and a large part of Western Europe: The Dark Ages.

The reason for Honorius' decision to withdraw all available Roman Briton legions back to Rome was due to a fearsome attack by the Visigoths on the empire's ancient capital city. Honorius had turned down an offer of peace with his enemies in exchange for regular payments, and he thereby brought on the wrath of the powerful Visigoth army. They attacked on August 24th, 410, and pillaged for three days within Rome's walls before leaving the city in a heap of smoking debris.[20] The Eastern Roman Empire, which had converted

---

[20] Kerrigan, Michael. "Sack of Rome." *Encyclopedia Britannica*. Web.

into the Byzantine Empire, still stood; the Western Roman Empire was heavily defeated, however, for the first time in 800 years.[21]

The remaining Roman soldiers and appointed leaders of the once-immense empire mostly retreated back to Italy to try to consolidate some measure of power on a much smaller scale. Roman governors, politicians, and industry leaders in Britannia did the same, leaving behind a large number of British-born Roman citizens. Fifth-century England still had its Roman-style cities, infrastructure, and culture, but it was abruptly cut off from many of its important continental trading partners. Without the regular trade England had enjoyed along the well-maintained and far-reaching Roman roads—both in Britannia and on the mainland—its infrastructure slowly fell into disrepair. With roads grown over and once-bustling trading forums nearly empty, the cities of Britannia shrank. The economy shifted drastically once more, as agriculture and regional rule returned to the land.

The following two centuries of English history are virtually nonexistent, as very few records seem to have been kept. There are many reasons this may be so, including the hypothesis that access to education had greatly fallen during that time. Furthermore, the languages of the land's oldest cultures had begun to intermingle with the Latin used in the newer cities, creating scripts that are illegible to modern linguists. Archaeologists have uncovered evidence that many of the forts originally built by the Romans were maintained for some time, including many along the length of Hadrian's Wall. It seems likely that many of Britannia's people, at least those with Roman heritage, made a considerable effort to continue the ways of the Romans. As time went on, though, this became more difficult, especially when they realized that the Roman Empire as they knew it had collapsed.

---

[21] Ibid.

Christianity appears to have been a part of post-Roman Britannia according to the archaeological record.[22] Roman Emperor Constantine the Great, who died in 337, had notoriously converted to Christianity during his reign, inspiring a wave of religious transformation that eventually encompassed most of the empire.[23] This religion had made its way to Britannia in the final century of Roman occupation, but it continued on, not only because Britons wanted to preserve their Roman culture but also because of the influx of other traders and immigrants from Germany, some of whom were also Christian. The religion was new and popular in many parts of Europe, and though it generally encroached violently upon the land, Britannia's transition was peaceful. In fact, a widespread desperation to preserve Roman culture may have fueled England's adoption of Christianity.

Once the famously impenetrable Roman army had been removed from Britannia, the people found themselves dealing with new political and economic situations. Just four decades after the fall of the Western Roman Empire, a local Kentish ruler named Vortigen, also spelled as Vortigern, decided to take matters into his own hands. He asked a group of Jute mercenaries from Denmark to come to Britannia and fight with him against the Picts and Scots, who had continued their attacks on Roman settlements throughout the occupation of the empire.[24] The mercenaries did as they were asked before turning on Vortigen and taking Kent for themselves. They established a new kingdom under their own selected leaders, named Hengist and Horsa. Hengist and Horsa may have been the first Saxon kings in England.[25]

---

[22] Petts, David. "Christianity in Roman Britain." *The Oxford Handbook of Roman Britain.* 2016.

[23] MacGillivray Nicol, Donald, and Matthews, J.F. "Constantine I." *Encyclopedia Britannica.*

[24] "The Dark Ages." *History of England.* Web.

[25] "The Dark Ages." *History of England.* Web.

Soon afterward, similar events resulted in the establishment of the Kingdoms of Sussex, Wessex, and Essex. The Kingdoms of Northumbria, East Anglia, and Mercia were similarly established by another Germanic tribe known as the Angles. By the 7th century, former Britannia was divided into seven separate Germanic kingdoms. The rulers of these kingdoms had violently ended the lives of most of the native Britons and Roman-descended Britons within reach, so the surviving members of these societies flocked to Wales, Scotland, and Cornwall. In Cornwall, a kingdom of Roman Britons was established. Around 200,000 Angles, Saxons, and Jutes are estimated to have lived in England at that point.[26] Thus began the Anglo-Saxon period of English history.

Though the new powerful inhabitants of the land had a common culture and ancestry, they were by no means peaceful with each other. Fighting between the newly established kingdoms was just as common as diplomatic missions and intermarriage. Having pushed aside the previous society as much as possible, the Anglo-Saxons made no attempts whatsoever to preserve anything of the Roman culture. After all, the Germanic tribes had been almost constantly at odds with the Roman Empire for centuries. Ethnically, the collective Anglo-Saxons were an amalgamation of Germanic tribes, and the inhabitants of each of the different kingdoms spoke distinctive dialects under a common language umbrella. These languages replaced Latin and evolved into a common Anglo-Saxon language that was used to create many works of great literature, including *Beowulf* and *Caedmon's Hymn*. It is also known as Old English.

Steadily, England began to look more like an Anglo-Saxon territory. Even many of the Roman-style stone buildings were destroyed in favor of the Germanic style of architecture, which primarily used wood. The Anglo-Saxons also had their own ancient religious beliefs, though many of them were also Christian. After the turn of

---

[26] Ibid.

the 7th century, a few years after Saint Augustine of Canterbury arrived in England, most of the land had converted to Christianity.

Once the new kingdoms were firmly established, two centuries of power shifts between Northumbria, Mercia, and Wessex followed. First, Northumbria took control of all of England except for Kent from the year 613 to 731.[27] King Edwin of Northumbria was convinced by his wife Æthelburh—also the daughter of the Christian king of Kent, Æthelberht—to become a Christian. His and other prominent Christian transformations rapidly turned England into a noted Christian land.

In 679, the majority of economic and military might was held by Mercia, and by 757, King Offa of Mercia was functionally the ruler of all England except for Northumbria. England firmly established its agricultural and mining industries to provide trade items with neighboring countries, including France. Noted for having a good relationship with King Charles the Great of France—also known as Charlemagne—King Offa introduced many continental-style systems into his own kingdom. These included a new currency, of which the coins boasted the same silver content as French coins, making them of equal value for trade. Military prowess and defense were also a primary focus for Offa, who commissioned a 26-foot-high, 120-mile-long rammed earth dike to keep indigenous Britons in Wales from attacking his communities.

Both Mercian and Northumbrian kings held a great deal of power over the following two centuries, with Wessex entering into the political landscape as well. King Egbert of Wessex proved the most powerful of all in the early 9th century when his military might surpassed that of the long-time powerhouse Mercia. Using this highly valuable resource, Egbert pacified the long-time Roman Briton holdout of Cornwall in the south, thereby greatly expanding his realm and influence. Furthermore, it is thought that Egbert married Charlemagne's sister and created a strong bond between his own kingdom and that of the Franks, although some historians dismiss this idea.

King Egbert created the Kingdom of Wessex, which had unprecedented power, a kingdom that was poised to unify all of England.

---

[27]Ibid.

Chapter Five – Alfred the Great

Alfred of Wessex was born to royal parents in the year 849, but as the youngest of many sons, he was not a king-in-training.[28] Eager to learn his letters and study Latin and poetry, young Alfred was given an education focused primarily on military skills. With Wessex and other kingdoms in constant danger of attacks from the Danes, it was important for Alfred and his three elder brothers to learn how to fight and manage battles. In 868, Alfred began his military service by the side of his brother, King Æthelred I.[29] They banded with the Kingdom of Mercia against a large army of Vikings who had landed in East Anglia three years earlier and taken over Northumbria. Though the combined English armies were prepared to fight, the Danes refused to do so, and instead, diplomatic meetings were arranged to make peace. This was the same year in which Alfred married a Mercian princess by the name of Ealhswith; this was a clever political move that would more closely align the two kingdoms in future endeavors.

---

[28] "Alfred 'the Great.'" *The Royal Family.* Web.

[29] McDermott, Gary. "Alfred the Great: Viking Wars and Military Reforms." *Academia.* 2009.

Though peace was won that particular day, the Danes were by no means finished with England. They had a culture of warfare and farming, and the invaders ultimately wanted to own their own homesteads somewhere on the British Isles. To this end, they invaded Wessex late in 871 to wage war against King Æthelred.[30] The king died in battle, and since his two elder brothers were also deceased, the crown fell to the unlikely Alfred.

As king of Wessex, Alfred's main concern was fending off Danish attacks. He marched into battle many times with his army, usually managing to win or at least draw up a peace agreement. There were notable battles in 876 and 878, during which Alfred won many cities.[31] Much of the kingdom was forced to submit to the raiders, but King Alfred refused to do so. He retreated to a bunker in Somerset Marsh and built up his army before leading it to victory in the Battle of Edington in May 878. Still determined to stay in England, Danish King Guthrum submitted to Alfred and was given land in East Anglia in exchange for his Christian baptism at the hand of Alfred.

King Guthrum's baptismal ceremony included King Alfred himself as his godfather. Afterward, the two worked together to find a solution to their dispute, and Alfred delineated a specific swath of land in East Anglia where the Danes were allowed to settle. Many returned to England thereafter and did indeed build homes and start family farms. This area was formally outlined in an 886 treaty signed by both parties; one of its borders ran along the old Roman Watling Road.[32] The treaty land was known as Danelaw, and it encompassed almost the entire eastern half of England. Therefore, Alfred took control of the western areas of Mercia and Kent, while King Guthrum took eastern Mercia and part of southern Northumbria.

---

[30] Ibid.

[31] "Battle of Edington." *Encyclopedia Britannica.* Web.

[32] "Alfred 'the Great.'" *The Royal Family.* Web.

Effectively, Kings Alfred and Guthrum split England between them, with just Wales and a small part of Northumbria set apart.

King Alfred did not blindly trust the word of his Danish counterpart once the country had been divided between them, and, though he remained ever diplomatic, Alfred focused his efforts on revamping the Wessex army. Knowing that the economic prosperity of his country depended on its security, Alfred created a rota system, in which soldiers could be summoned quickly, but some would be left behind to continue tending the fields. Though relations with the Danes remained positive, other groups of Vikings continued to sail to England in search of plunder. They pillaged many of England's monasteries in search of the gold and jewels that were kept there. This destruction not only frustrated King Alfred's efforts to maintain a strong and stoic Catholic nation but also his desire for England to be a nation of highly educated clergy.

To improve the educational facilities in his kingdom, Alfred personally expanded his own knowledge of foreign languages so that he could help translate texts held in high esteem in other parts of Europe, particularly France. These texts covered a variety of topics, including history, geography, philosophy, and administration. He also patronized the *Anglo-Saxon Chronicle*, a historical work that began with the roots of Wessex and painted both the kingdom and King Alfred in a benevolent light. The book would continue to be added to for at least another three centuries afterward.

One of Alfred's personal works was the translation of Saint Gregory the Great's *Pastoral Care*. Saint Gregory the Great was a 7th-century pope whose personal mission was to convert England's Anglo-Saxons to Christianity. His book, *Pastoral Care*, was something of a guidebook for members of the clergy in caring for their communities.

In King Alfred's translation, the king wrote the following in its preface:

...it very often comes to my mind what wise men there formerly were throughout England, both of sacred and secular orders; and how happy the times were then throughout England; and how the kings who then had power over the people obeyed God and his ministers; and they maintained their peace, their morality and their power within their borders, and also increased their kingdom without; and how they prospered both with war and with wisdom; and also how eager the sacred orders were about both teaching and learning, and about all the services that they ought to do for God; and how men from abroad came to this land in search of wisdom and teaching, and how we now must get them from abroad if we shall have them. So completely had wisdom fallen off in England that there were very few on this side of the Humber who could understand their rituals in English, or indeed could translate a letter from Latin into English; and I believe that there were not many beyond the Humber. There were so few of them that I indeed cannot think of a single one south of the Thames when I became king. Thanks be to God almighty that we now have any supply of teachers. Therefore I command you to do as I believe you are willing to do, that you free yourself from worldly affairs as often as you can, so that wherever you can establish that wisdom that God gave you, you establish it. Consider what punishments befell us in this world when we neither loved wisdom at all ourselves, nor transmitted it to other men; we had the name alone that we were Christians, and very few had the practices.[33]

King Alfred was saddened at how England had lost so much of its former knowledge and culture, and he endeavored to help return some of it to the kingdom he ruled. Part of his studies into England's past was to translate this very book from Latin into contemporary

---

[33] "Translation of Alfred's Prose Preface to Pastoral Care." *Bucknell University.* Web.

English and to send a copy to each of his country's bishops. For his meticulous work in dealing with external and internal threats to Wessex, expanding his kingdom to encompass at least half of modern England, and organizing his realm to more efficiently provide labor, goods, and warriors, Alfred the Great guaranteed the continuation of his royal family line for generations to come.

Chapter Six – Danelaw

Through a series of conquests that took place outside of the Danes' treaty with Anglo-Saxon King Alfred, the Danish settlers were able to maintain a massive portion of England. Incoming bands of Vikings made their own agreements with the kings of Danelaw, thereby expanding the population of the region. Though the Danes did not settle the entire span of Danelaw, they nevertheless cultivated a great deal of respect from their neighbors due to their military achievements. As the name of the region suggests, Danelaw was under the authority of its own leaders and laws.

King Guthrum, after making his bargain with King Alfred, changed his name to Æthelstan upon converting to Christianity and settled in a southern stretch of Danelaw he called the Kingdom of Guthrum. To the east, where the king of Mercia had been driven out by the Vikings, there was Danish Mercia. This came under the rule of five different Danish armies who established five towns as their political bases: Derby, Leicester, Lincoln, Nottingham, and Stamford. These were called the Five Boroughs, and each city was surrounded by a fortified wall to keep residents safely inside.

Many administrative differences existed between the Anglo-Saxons and the Danes of England, including the presence of a large number of working peasants who were loyal to their lord. For the Anglo-Saxons, peasants were attached to the land they worked, while Danish peasants could move about much more freely. The latter were called *sokemen*.[34] Keeping the peace was an important facet within these Danish boroughs, and failing to follow the letters of Danish law meant facing a committee of local aristocrats who were responsible for doling out punishments or deciding if the accused should be released.

York was the capital of all of Danelaw, and it would remain so for over seven decades following its successful invasion by the army of Viking leader Halfdan Ragnarsson, potentially the son of the legendary Viking King Ragnar Lodbrok. In fact, it was Lodbrok's death at the hands of King Ælla of Northumbria that gave the sons of Ragnar reason to attack Northumbria in the first place. Having done so in the name of their father, Halfdan and his brother Ivar the Boneless settled for nothing less than the total control of Northumbria. While Ivar went on to conquer Ireland's capital and earned the title "King of Dublin," Halfdan stayed on in York and went on to lead an unsuccessful attack against Wessex. He died in 877, attempting to reclaim the Irish territory of his dead brother Ivar.[35]

Halfdan was succeeded by another Viking called Guthfrith; the latter died a few years later and was eventually replaced by Rægnald. Rægnald, heralded as a grandson of Ivar the Boneless, fought the Scots to the north of York and won control of all of northern

---

[34] "Danelaw." *Encyclopedia Britannica.* Web.

[35] *Annals of Ulster.* Retrieved from CELT: Corpus of Electronic Texts at University College Cork. The Corpus of Electronic Texts includes the Annals of Ulster and the Four Masters, the Chronicon Scotorum and the Book of Leinster as well as Genealogies, and various Saints' Lives. Most are translated into English, or translations are in progress.

England in 916. [36] Satisfied with the kingdom he had amassed for himself and his people, Rægnald pledged loyalty to the Anglo-Saxon King Edward the Elder—the son of King Alfred—in 921. [37] This peace agreement between the Vikings and Anglo-Saxons was a wise move on the part of Rægnald since King Edward had taken impressive strides in removing pieces of Danelaw from Viking control and adding them back to his own domain.

King Edward inherited the throne of Wessex after the death of his father Alfred in 899. [38] His crown was not secure, however, and to maintain the throne, Edward was thrown into battle with his own cousin and would-be usurper, Æthelwold. Æthelwold was an ally of the Danes and Vikings, whereas Edward intended to remove as many Vikings from the land as he could manage with his powerful army. Æthelwold was killed in battle in 902, leaving Edward to move forward with his political goals. [39] He took his time in gathering and training soldiers before testing them out against the Danes in Northumbria in 912, and he came back victorious. He set to building a collection of fortifications around Wessex from 910 to about 916, and when his defenses and army were properly prepared, he began a series of attacks on the strongholds of Danelaw.

King Edward was not alone in his efforts. Queen Æthelflæd of Mercia, the king's sister, commanded her own complementary military strategies alongside her brother, fortifying much of the English Midlands. Following her husband's death in 911, Æthelflæd was honored with the very rare title of Queen of Mercia. Also called the Lady of the Mercians, Æthelflæd led military campaigns multiple times to protect her kingdom from Viking raiders. In 917, she and

---

[36] "The Viking Kings of York." *English Monarchs*. Web. 2018.

[37] Ibid.

[38] "Edward, Anglo-Saxon King." *Encyclopedia Britannica*. Web.

[39] Ibid.

Edward launched an attack on Danish East Anglia that was a huge success.[40] The very next year, the Vikings of Leicester surrendered to the queen without fighting a single battle. Though the *Anglo-Saxon Chronicle* hardly deigns to mention the exploits of the Lady of the Mercians—probably due to their entirely male-centered culture—the *Mercian Register* gives an account of her many deeds.

Upon Æthelflæd's death from illness in June 918, Edward assumed control of Mercia, and by the end of the year, the last Danish armies in the Midlands had submitted.[41] As Wessex grew, King Edward kept on pushing to clear the land of the Vikings, and in 920, he forced the submission of Northumbria.[42] During the reign of Edward's son and successor, King Æthelstan, the total unification of England was finally achieved. Æthelstan was the first ruler to use the title "King of the English," and on the silver coins minted under his authority were printed the Latin words REX TOTIUS BRITANNIAE, MEANING "King of all Britain."[43]

---

[40] Ibid.

[41] Ibid.

[42] Ibid

[43] "Athelstan, King of England." *Encyclopedia Britannica.* Web.

Chapter Seven – The Norman Conquest

Normandy lay just across the English Channel, south from England, and just a short distance from the Kingdom of the Franks. The land proved compelling to the Vikings of the early 10th century, and in 911, King Charles III of West Francia had little choice but to offer it to the most powerful and dangerous band of Vikings he had encountered.[44] Those Vikings were led by Rollo, and under his authority, they happily accepted the land around modern France's northwestern coastline. Rollo's people sent for their families and settled in the region permanently, learning to conduct themselves in the French manner and speak French among one another. They were called the Northmen, and they eventually became known as the Normans, and their land became known as Normandy.

Normandy had close political ties with England in the 11th century due to intermarriage between the two kingdoms. The mother of King Edward the Confessor of England was Norman, so, therefore, the king had cousins across the Channel. During a time of political uncertainty in his youth, Edward was even sent to live in Normandy

---

[44] "Normandy." *Encyclopedia Britannica.* Web.

until he was old enough to safely rejoin his family at the English court. When Edward became king of England in 1042, he invited several of his Norman companions to join him at court, which created jealousy among the powerful Mercia and Wessex families.

Unwisely, King Edward the Confessor promised to leave his crown to several potential heirs. Since he did not have children of his own, he could have potentially named William, Duke of Normandy, as his successor. Probably in preparation for his ascension, William married Matilda of Flanders, a descendant of King Alfred the Great. Unfortunately for William, it seems that King Edward made a similar promise of inheritance to Harold Godwinson, Earl of Wessex.

On his deathbed on January 5th, 1066, King Edward's will was in favor of Harold succeeding him, and he was crowned the very next day. This was problematic for William of Normandy since Harold had previously agreed to support his own bid for the crown of England. Furthermore, Harold's brother, Tostig, and King Harald III Hardrada of Norway had also set their sights on England's throne. As soon as King Harold II of England was pronounced king of England, his enemies began to move in, starting with his brother Tostig.

In the early summer of 1066, Tostig ran raids across southern and eastern England. Harold II managed to hold them off throughout the warm months but was forced to disband his army when supplies ran low and the farmers needed to tend to harvesting their fields. Little time passed before Tostig and Harald Hardrada decided to join forces against Harold II. On September 25th, the two sides met in Yorkshire, where they fought a decisive battle at Stamford Bridge. Both would-be usurpers were killed by Harold II's forces, leaving only William of Normandy for the English king to contend with.

William landed in southeast England with several thousand soldiers just three days after the battle at Stamford Bridge. With about the same number of soldiers, King Harold II made haste southward to meet his final enemy at Hastings on October 14th.[45] After many hours of ferocious battle, the king of England caught an arrow in the eye and was killed, although there is some disagreement as to how he actually died. Still, those loyal to him fought for several more hours before finally turning to flee.

William moved on to claim London and was met by various political leaders there, who submitted to him. He was crowned king of England on Christmas Day, 1066. His political changes to the kingdom would resonate for a millennium and greatly influence how future English monarchs organized and ruled their realm. William's rule was largely characterized by the building of many large, impenetrable castles, such as London's White Tower. He also enacted an immense reshuffling of land holdings throughout the kingdom, ensuring that his own Norman family members and loyal supporters became the most important landlords of the realm. As a consequence of this, French became the primary language of the English court.

Twenty years after seizing the throne, King William I of England—also called William the Conqueror—came into danger once more from would-be usurpers of the throne. This time, the threat came from King Canute IV of Denmark. It became necessary for William I to consolidate all of his available fighting men and resources to wage a proper defense. Knowing that he would require mercenary soldiers, William also knew that he needed to find the money to pay for them. Unfortunately, the king was unsure just what his resources were since there were no records detailing such an inventory. So, William demanded that a detailed inventory be taken of all the English lands, public and private. That great undertaking would become the Domesday Book. The book itself was not named as such, but it quickly earned the moniker "Domesday" as a metaphor for the biblical book of judgment.

---

[45] "Norman Conquest." *Encyclopedia Britannica.* Web.

To complete the Domesday Book, a great many surveyors were required. These surveyors conducted a very thorough inventory of the kingdom, down to the number of pigs owned by each household. They set out to record all items of value located in every town and manor. William's wishes were clear-cut: he wanted to know who owned what and how much each estate or town owed him in taxes or service. It also notes which manors belonged to which landowner and which noblemen owed him military service as a knight.

The book, written in Medieval Latin, had some additions in vernacular Anglo-Saxon and Norman-style French. These, as well as many abbreviations, has made the translation of the book quite difficult, but it certainly served its purpose well enough for King William. His inventory not only allowed him to calculate the value of future taxes on his kingdom, but his surveyors also collected sums that had been owed to King Edward the Confessor upon his death. Therefore, William found a large amount of financial support for his defense against Denmark.

Fortunately for William I, King Canute IV was killed by rebels before William could so much as set sail from mainland Europe, where he spent much of his time. England was once more in the hands of the Normans, and it would remain so for over half a century.

Chapter Eight – Magna Carta

John of Angevin became the king of England in 1199 after his brother, King Richard I, was killed in France. Both John and Richard were direct descendants of William I, though additions to the family tree meant that they now represented the House of Plantagenet, sometimes also known as Anjou. The majority of John's rule was focused on the reclamation of Normandy and other lands on the continent that had previously been under English authority. While war constantly raged in France, John struggled to rule over a chaotic patchwork of administrative regions that could be very unpredictable. His was a violent reign, and the use of force exercised by King John to take what he needed from his people was justified by his belief that he was above the law.

Following another attempt to win French lands back without success in 1215, John had to sue his enemy for peace. France demanded compensation that bankrupted the English king. When John returned from France, he found that the rebel barons had formed an allied opposition to his rule in the north and east of England. His crown and life were in jeopardy since these united families controlled a great deal of land. The rebels were members of the nobility, and as such, they were considered to be local leaders in their counties. If their will was to hunt the king with an army and have him replaced, such a thing could be done.

In defense of King John, Pope Innocent III wrote several letters ascertaining that John was the legal and rightful ruler of England. The letters proved ineffective with the rebels, particularly because by that time, the nobles had banded together and had begun raising an army. The king's only viable option was diplomacy, and though this was not his strong suit, King John met with the protestors at Northampton to discuss an agreement. To his credit, John was largely successful in his effort to appear moderate and conciliatory, but the meeting was of no use. The rebels moved into London and took it for their cause, at which time many more people joined their brigade.

When offered another meeting with the pope as their sole arbitrator, the rebels refused in favor of the Archbishop of Canterbury, Stephen Langton. Langton, who had already been carrying on a dialogue with the militant group, agreed to help create a formal contract between the people of England and the king. To that end, the royalists and the rebels met again at a meadow on the southern side of the River Thames, called Runnymede, on June 10th, 1215.[46] There, the rebels presented King John with "The Articles of the Barons," which was a rough list of their demands. With the help of the Archbishop of Canterbury, these demands were amended into the formal document that would eventually be referred to as the Magna Carta, or "Great Document."

Some of the key clauses of the agreement are as follows:

> JOHN, by the grace of God King of England, Lord of Ireland, Duke of Normandy and Aquitaine, and Count of Anjou, to his archbishops, bishops, abbots, earls, barons,

---

[46] "Timeline of Magna Carta and its Legacy." *British Library.* Web. 28 July 2014.

justices, foresters, sheriffs, stewards, servants, and to all his officials and loyal subjects, Greeting.

If any earl, baron, or other person that holds lands directly of the Crown, for military service, shall die, and at his death his heir shall be of full age and owe a "relief," the heir shall have his inheritance on payment of the ancient scale of "relief."

Neither we nor our officials will seize any land or rent in payment of a debt, so long as the debtor has movable goods sufficient to discharge the debt.

No free man shall be seized or imprisoned, or stripped of his rights or possessions, or outlawed or exiled, or deprived of his standing in any way, nor will we proceed with force against him, or send others to do so, except by the lawful judgment of his equals or by the law of the land.

We give and grant to the barons the following security: The barons shall elect twenty-five of their number to keep, and cause to be observed with all their might, the peace and liberties granted and confirmed to them by this charter.[47]

The Magna Carta's first clause guarantees the English Church's independence from the king. That rule was intended specifically to stop the king from interfering with what the Church was doing and giving the Church the right to elect its own members instead of the king selecting them. The appointment of the Archbishop of Canterbury had been in the hands of King John and the pope, and the first provision of the new document was meant to make sure that the difficulties over who would be in these key positions would not arise anymore. The significance of this piece of the Magna Carta shows how much power and significance the Catholic Church held in ancient England. It also demonstrates why England's churches were so defensive of the Magna Carta in the years after it was signed.

---

[47] "English translation of Magna Carta." *British Library.* Web. 28 July 2014.

King John did indeed sign the document after a week of conferences with both parties and the Archbishop of Canterbury. The general purpose of the Magna Carta was to lower the king's power to take what money, people, and lands he wanted from his citizens. As for King John, he received the renewed loyalty—at least on paper—of his noble barons.

Mere weeks later, King John complained to Pope Innocent III that the charter had jeopardized the status of the pope himself in England. Meanwhile, the pope's letters finally arrived in which he proclaimed all the rebel lords to be excommunicated from the Church. He also removed Langdon from his post. Once made aware of the proceedings between Langdon, the rebels, and the king, Pope Innocent responded that the deal was not only disgraceful but completely illegal. Furthermore, the barons were meant to surrender London by August 15th as part of the June peace agreement, which they did not follow through on.

With neither party interested in meeting the stipulations of their own agreement, England dissolved into civil war. The very next year, King John died of dysentery while the war raged on in the eastern part of the kingdom. His son, Henry, only nine years old, inherited the heavy crown of England in October 1216.[48] Royal forces eventually prevailed over the combined armies of the barons and their French supporters in 1217, but there was still an uncomfortable coexistence between the nobles and the royal house. In 1225, King Henry III agreed to abide by a new version of the document his father had signed. Called the Great Charter, this document called for less royal power and the protection of the rights of the most influential barons. It would be the most highly touted piece of legislation in England for centuries to come.

---

[48] "Henry III." *Encyclopedia Britannica.* Web.

Chapter Nine – The Black Death

As the population of England and Europe grew in leaps and bounds throughout the Middle Ages, so, too, did the people's risk of contracting deadly diseases. Personal hygiene was virtually unknown during the early medieval period in England, and without soap, people used their own urine to launder clothes and other textiles. Without handwashing, regular bathing, clean water to drink, and knowledge of cleanly cooking habits, people were surrounded by filth, bacteria, and terrible odors. Infections were very common, and even the simplest injury could potentially become deadly due to a lack of proper care. Viruses and diseases spread easily, but in earlier centuries, there had been nothing like the deadly sickness that made its way to England in the mid-14th century.

Though no one is certain exactly how the plague first reached England, or whether it first stepped onshore aboard an infected rat or sick person, the first news the English people received of the sickness was in 1347.[49] According to sources from abroad, there was a horrible, deadly, and incurable disease spreading from Asia to

---

[49] "London plagues 1348–1665." *Museum of London.* Web.

North Africa and Europe. Just a year later, in the autumn of 1348, London was struck by that same disease.[50] Over the next year and a half, an estimated half of all Londoners were killed by the pestilence—that is potentially 40,000 people.[51] There were many names given to the terrible sickness that afflicted so many during this period, including the "Great Death," but the most formidable and lasting name would be "The Black Death," a term that wasn't in use until the 17th century.

The path of the original strain of plague seems to have first struck the south of England in the summer of 1348 before moving north with the colder weather.[52] The sickness hit London first in September, and it soon moved onto East Anglia and along the coast in the first months of 1349.[53] In the spring, the plague could be found in the Midlands and Wales, and by summer, it was across the Irish Sea. As for Scotland, the northern nation was evidently unbothered by the plague until 1350, which may or may not have had something to do with the Scottish raid south of the border on Durham the previous year.[54]

The plague presented itself in a variety of ways on different victims. Generally, the first symptom of infection was a large swollen area on the surface of the skin. These were lymph nodes, where the bulk of bacteria was carried, and in a matter of hours, the infection swelled to painful proportions. The bubonic plague, so named because of these painful "buboes" of the armpits, groin, or neck, passed between fleas and their victims. The buboes turned orange, then dark purple or black, and death came in a matter of days due to the

---

[50] Ibid.

[51] Ibid.

[52] Ibeji, Dr. Mike. "Black Death." *BBC*. Web. 2011.

[53] Ibid.

[54] Ibid.

infection spreading into the victim's bloodstream. In some cases, the infection spread into the lungs and was coughed and sneezed out by its victims. In these cases, infection between people was possible, which was known as the pneumonic plague.

In the streets of London, there were so many dead from the disease that they were consigned to be buried in mass graves together. There was no time nor space for rituals or offering respect for the dead; bodies were dealt with as quickly as possible to keep away the stench of rotting corpses. In some places, such as a mass grave unearthed by archaeologists at the Royal Mint near the Tower of London, bodies were piled up five high, with smaller children's bodies squashed into the crevices between adults.[55] By 1350, the Black Death had killed millions of people, forever changing the shape and future of England.[56]

In an effort to explain why the disease had struck so violently, philosophers and physicians alike pondered whether it was a punishment from God, either upon individuals or England as a nation. Some wondered if the sickness had been foretold in the stars, a malignant result of evil planetary alignment or star movements. Some even speculated that those of the Jewish faith were somehow poisoning Christians; in fact, this was believed by enough people to inspire incidents of genocide against the Jewish people living in England. To people whose lives revolved around religion, watching so many family members, friends, and neighbors suffer and die seemed like the beginning of the end of the world. The survivors and the sick talked of Armageddon, while many were panicked and overcome by mania.

The pace of the epidemic in the medieval world was frightening. Though it is believed that the symptoms of the plague took about seven days to appear, once a bubo was sighted, there was sometimes

---

[55] Ibid.

[56] Ibid.

only a matter of hours left in a victim's life. As the people died in the thousands, a labor shortage grew that was difficult to deal with. On farms, heavy rains and dwindling farmers meant that while some crops were neglected altogether, others rotted in the ground. Soon, there was not only a shortage of workers but a shortage of food to go around. The survivors struggled to feed themselves, which meant that there was now a population of weak immune systems upon which the plague could continue to prey.

Many people, gripped by fear, began to do public penance as a way to ask God for forgiveness for whatever they might have done wrong to bring on the disease. Some of these people chose to whip themselves in view of their neighbors and families, earning themselves the collective name "Flagellators."[57] The more zealous of these people dressed in white robes and roamed the country carrying a large cross and whipping themselves bloody. Sir Robert of Avesbury, a contemporary Englishman who witnessed this ritual, wrote the following report:

> In that same year of 1349, about Michaelmas (September, 29) over six hundred men came to London from Flanders, mostly of Zeeland and Holland origin. Sometimes at St Paul's and sometimes at other points in the city they made two daily public appearances wearing cloths from the thighs to the ankles, but otherwise stripped bare. Each wore a cap marked with a red cross in front and behind.
>
> Each had in his right hand a scourge with three tails. Each tail had a knot and through the middle of it there were sometimes sharp nails fixed. They marched naked in a file one behind the other and whipped themselves with these scourges on their naked and bleeding bodies.[58]

---

[57] "The Flagellants Attempt to Repeal the Black Death, 1349." *EyeWitness to History.* Web. 2010.

[58] Reprinted in "The Flagellants Attempt to Repeal the Black Death, 1349." *EyeWitness to History.* Web. 2010.

In a year, the numbers of the dead and dying had begun to fall, but the original plague outbreak did not abate significantly for another century. As a result of the serious blow to England's population, the labor shortage hit a crisis point, so therefore, the entire economic system began to change. Land that had traditionally been used for farming was left to grow over, and more grazing animals were introduced to the pastures. Wages dropped sharply just as prices rose. Lawmakers attempted to force a return to pre-plague wages, but the economy was so unbalanced that this proved to be impossible. Landowners began renting their lands and homes out for income, and many people moved in order to find a relatively prosperous nearby urban center with decent jobs available.

Even once the first outbreak slowed down and seemed to abate, England was not free of the plague. Following 1348, there was another major outbreak of the plague every two or three decades, and every time it struck, about twenty percent of London's population was wiped out. Between the major occurrences of pestilence, the bacteria still took lives, just on a smaller scale. Of course, modern germ theory would not exist until the 19th century, and therefore, nobody could understand where the sickness came from or how it was spreading. No useful medicines existed to counteract such acute and powerful infections within the body, and so, plague victims often died after a great deal of suffering. The number of infected victims was always worse in the heat of the summer, especially in crowded urban areas like London.

The royal family and other wealthy aristocrats who could afford to leave the city made a habit of doing so before the plague season hit each summer. These lucky few retreated to the relative safety of the isolated countryside, where infection rates were low, as minimal social interactions kept the germs at bay. As for the poor of the cities who could neither afford to stop work nor find affordable accommodations outside of their own homes, they simply had to stay put and pray for God's protection.

The devastation of the Black Death was so great that it began to unravel the economic backbone of early medieval society, known as feudalism. Landlords had little choice but to allow their indentured servants leave to roam the countryside, looking for food, shelter, and jobs. In this small way, the plague forced England's society to rearrange itself in such a way that fewer and fewer of the country's poorest citizens would live a life of forced service.

Chapter Ten – The Tudor Dynasty

The royal Tudor dynasty began on August 22nd, 1485, when Henry Tudor and his supporters won the Battle of Bosworth Field. Henry was the nephew to the deceased King Henry VI of House Lancaster, and though he had a somewhat distant connection to the crown, he found a great deal of support in winning it with the help of his mother, Lady Margaret Beaufort. The victory at Bosworth Field against the York King Richard III marked the end of the ongoing Wars of the Roses, in which two competing factions of the royal family, the Yorks and the Lancasters, had struggled to assert their dominance.

Henry VII was technically the closest in relation to the Lancasters, so one of his first points of business as the new king was to formally unite both sides of the broken family with a wedding. He married Elizabeth of York, the niece of the former York King Edward IV, and hedged his bets on speedily producing an heir with mixed blood to inherit the throne. The deed was accomplished in September of the very next year, with the birth of Arthur, Prince of Wales. With that, the red rose emblem that represented the Lancasters and the white rose emblem that represented the Yorks were blended into the Tudor rose of both colors.

The country that King Henry VII won was a tumultuous one, one in which there was a great deal of power in the hands of the nobility and relatively little in the hands of the ruling monarch. During the previous thirty years, five kings had been placed on the throne of England, and many of those had been able to usurp power entirely because of the backing of rich noble families whose armies and funds cleared the path. Henry VII's own victory was due to such political maneuvering, and so to prevent the endless parade of monarchs from continuing, he rearranged how power was held throughout the kingdom.

Henry created new noble families whose loyalty was strong to the king to help bolster his position among the wealthy families of the realm. In addition, he created a system of local government in which each municipality of England was administrated by a justice of the peace and a sheriff, both of whom Henry personally appointed. Though previous monarchs had ruled through the same methods, the system had broken down completely over the course of the Wars of the Roses, and thus, Henry VII put an immense amount of energy and resources into its reestablishment. In regions where the king did not trust the family in power, he used a variety of methods to replace that family with one whose loyalty he did not question. Henry also arranged it so that the member of authority in a region was not actually a majority landholder there.

King Henry's marriage is considered to have been a success, not only because it knitted together two warring factions of the royal Plantagenet line but also because husband and wife were reportedly very fond of each other. They had four children together: Arthur, Margaret, Henry, and Mary. Arthur, Prince of Wales, was raised to become the next Tudor king, and he and his siblings received a good education in preparation for their adulthood in royal or political families abroad. They were brought up in the Catholic faith, as had been traditional for monarchs and nobles of England since the rule of King Alfred the Great in the 9th century.

Despite sharing a religion, England and Spain were on uncertain terms with one another during this period, which is why Henry VII arranged for his eldest son to marry a Spanish princess, Catherine of Aragon. The betrothed wrote letters to one another in their common language, Latin, as was the style in Europe during the Renaissance period. The letters were pleasant and loving, and when the pair finally married, both around the age of fifteen, in 1501, theirs was a happy union.[59]

Unfortunately, both the newlyweds contracted a serious illness when they embarked upon their new home together in Ludlow. Catherine recovered, but Arthur succumbed five months after the wedding. Henry VII was devastated at the sudden loss of his son and heir, and he shut himself away in private rooms for months trying to deal with his grief. The depression was compounded when Queen Elizabeth died the very next year.

When he emerged from mourning, Henry VII was a more solemn man but still very capable. Still intent on cultivating a good relationship with Spain, King Henry VII eventually decided that his younger son Henry should marry Catherine so that she still could be the queen of England. Henry agreed, and they were married seven years after the death of Arthur in 1509.[60] The wedding followed the death of King Henry VII and Henry VIII's subsequent coronation, which occurred right on the cusp of his eighteenth birthday.

King Henry VIII would become an astoundingly curious part of history due to his determination to divorce his wife after more than twenty years of marriage. Indeed, he went as far as to break England's connection to the Catholic Church, declaring himself to be

---

[59] "14 November 1501." *The Anne Boleyn Files.* Web. 2014.

[60] *Lehman, H. Eugene. Lives of England's Reigning and Consort Queens. 2011.*

the head of the Church of England, just to legitimize his divorce. The Reformation of England's principal religion occurred in 1533, the same year that King Henry VIII married for a second time to a Protestant member of a pro-Reformation family, Anne Boleyn.

The new marriage was largely desired by the king because he was desperate for a son; Catherine of Aragon had been pregnant multiple times but only delivered one healthy child, Mary Tudor. Anne Boleyn was Henry's new hope for a boy, and as he did not believe that females should inherit the throne, this was of the utmost importance to him. The king was very pleased when his young new wife became pregnant, which probably happened before the wedding actually took place, as she delivered a baby only six months after the ceremony. According to some sources, however, a secret wedding had already taken place in November of 1532.[61]

The birth of Elizabeth Tudor was much heralded, though, to her father and the expectant kingdom, her sex was a disappointment. On Anne's shoulders lay a huge responsibility over which she had no control: the task of conceiving and birthing boys. When a baby girl appeared on September 7th, 1533, it was all the more reason for the Catholics of England and all of Europe to condemn King Henry VIII for his disposal of Catholic law.[62] For the reformers of England, the girl signified a weakness in their cause.

Three years later, Anne had not given birth again, and the king had lost his interest in her altogether. This time, instead of a long and drawn-out divorce, he had Anne tried for treason, and she was executed at the Tower of London in 1536. Henry VIII did not return to Catholicism, however, as he had had his fill of following the will of any authority other than himself. He still wrote on the subject of God and the new religion, believing very much in the truth of what

---

[61] "14 November 1532 – The Marriage of Henry VIII and Anne Boleyn?" *The Anne Boleyn Files*. 2014.

[62] "Elizabeth I." *Encyclopedia Britannica*. Web.

he was preaching. Over the course of his lifetime, Henry VIII married six times. During his third marriage to Jane Seymour, he fathered a son named Edward. Jane died shortly after her son was born and was followed by three more wives. In all, Henry divorced two women and executed another two.

Marriages and the Reformation were not the only things that King Henry VIII accomplished, though these are certainly the most lasting impressions of his rule. During his reign, Henry also invested heavily in building up the navy with large sailing ships that were equipped with guns. England had depended greatly on its naval prowess in the days of the Viking conquests, but by the early Renaissance, its collection of sea-worthy vessels and able sailors had dwindled. Since Henry was a war-minded king, it made sense to funnel the money he appropriated by disbanding the Catholic churches and monasteries and seizing their goods and lands into the navy and his armies.

Unfortunately, overall, Henry's exploits in France were unsuccessful. He dreamed of reclaiming the country lost to Henry VI before the Wars of the Roses, but by the time he died, not even the long-time holdout of Calais was under English rule. Nevertheless, Henry had better luck in the British Isles, overseeing the legal unification of Ireland and Wales with England. Wales had been a very close ally for centuries, and as the Tudor family originally came from Wales, Henry had little opposition to this particular agreement. In 1542, Henry became the first English king to rule Ireland, following the Crown of Ireland Act.[63]

The last political holdout from English power within the British Isles was Scotland. Unable to win his northern neighbor by means of invasion, Henry VIII devised a marital scheme to join the two kingdoms together. English armies had killed King James V of Scotland during a Scottish invasion the same year Henry signed

---

[63] "Crown of Ireland Act 1542." *Heraldica*. Web.

unification treaties with Wales and Ireland, leaving only James' infant daughter Mary as the heir. Henry saw his opportunity to marry his own son Edward to Mary, thereby tying Scotland into the union by marital law. The plan bore no fruit, however, and when Henry VIII died in 1547, Edward inherited the crown as an unmarried nine-year-old boy.[64]

Though Edward VI died at the age of fifteen, he managed to contribute a great deal of work to the Church of England. He worked extensively with Thomas Cranmer, the Archbishop of Canterbury, in creating English-language texts for use in the churches. These included *An English Prayer Book* and the *Book of Common Prayer*, which would become fundamental bases for the Anglican Church. Just before his death from an unknown illness, King Edward VI willed his crown to his young cousin, Jane Grey, knowing that she was also a devout Anglican who would protect all he had done for the Church of England during his short reign. Unfortunately, Jane was forcibly deposed after only nine days by Edward's elder half-sister, Mary Tudor.

Mary was the daughter of Henry VIII's first wife, Catherine of Aragon, and she was staunchly Catholic—probably the very reason that Edward had not selected her as his successor. Her tumultuous reign lasted five years and was characterized by excessive violence and unrest. Though at first Mary promised her parliament that she would respect the rights of England's Protestant majority, it soon became clear that she preferred to reinstate England as a Catholic kingdom. She had hundreds of Protestants burned at the stake as heretics when they refused to convert to Catholicism. This earned her the timeless nickname "Bloody Mary."

Mary I died childless in 1558, at which point Elizabeth Tudor was made Queen of England. She promised leniency for Catholics but returned England officially to Anglicanism under the Church of

---

[64] "Henry VIII." *Encyclopedia Britannica.* Web.

England, using the texts her brother had helped create. It should be noted that Elizabeth also killed hundreds for religious reasons, a fact that is often overshadowed by her elder half-sister's moniker. Under Elizabeth I, the navy her grandfather had founded developed into England's major defense and became the means by which the British Empire was extended around the globe.

From the beginning of her reign, Queen Elizabeth I was urged on all sides to find a husband and to do so quickly. Naturally, she worried that in doing so she would not just be selecting a husband but a king of England who would usurp her powers. She rebelled, addressing her parliament and beseeching them for respect in her own rights and not as a placeholder for a male ruler. She assured them that in time she would find a husband, if only to produce children, and asked for their patience. The following passage is from one of Elizabeth's official speeches to her government:

> Was I not born in the realm? Were my parents born in any foreign country? Is not my kingdom here? Whom have I oppressed? Whom have I enriched to other's harm? What turmoil have I made in this commonwealth that I should be suspected to have no regard to the same? How have I governed since my reign? I will be tried by envy itself. I need not to use many words, for my deeds do try me.

> Well, the matter whereof they would have made their petition (as I am informed) consisteth in two points: in my marriage, and in the limitations of the succession of the crown, wherein my marriage was first placed, as for manners' sake. I did send them answer by my council, I would marry (although of mine own disposition I was not inclined thereunto) but that was not accepted nor credited, although spoken by their Prince.

> I will never break the word of a prince spoken in a public place, for my honour's sake. And therefore I say again, I will marry as soon as I can conveniently, if God take not him away with whom I mind to marry, or myself, or else some

other great let happen. I can say no more except the party were present. And I hope to have children, otherwise I would never marry. A strange order of petitioners that will make a request and cannot be otherwise assured but by the prince's word, and yet will not believe it when it is spoken.[65]

Queen Elizabeth I never did marry. She did, however, enjoy a long, prosperous reign that has often been called the Golden Age of England.

[65] "Elizabeth I of England Speeches (1566-1601)." *Hanover College History Department.* Web.

Chapter Eleven – England's Diaspora

Queen Elizabeth I was less interested in accounts of the new lands of America than she was with more pressing matters, such as the continual attempts of Spain to attack England's southern coast. Nevertheless, she could not ignore the fact that so many of her European neighbors were positioning themselves to capitalize on American goods, trade, and colonization. With Spain, France, Portugal, and the Netherlands all making big gains in the New World, the queen decided to set her main focus eastward toward India. Her primary goal was to establish England as the main source of trade with India and its exotic teas and spices. Although that was her main focus, she still gave permission for two men to begin the colonization of America on her behalf.

The queen began her colonial enterprise during the 1570s and 1580s. England's priority was on America's northeastern coast since she knew Spain's colonies were in the south; so, being in the northeastern region would make it easier to find a stronghold there. To that end, Elizabeth's chosen captain, Sir Humphrey Gilbert, made three long voyages and started three colonies. Each of these failed, and Humphrey himself was lost at sea on his final return trip in 1583.[66] Not yet ready to concede defeat, Elizabeth granted Gilbert's patent to his half-brother, Sir Walter Raleigh. The patent came with the rights to much of the land Raleigh would find there, which had first been promised to Gilbert.

Walter Raleigh was many things besides a sailor: he was also an author, a soldier, and he considered himself an adventurer. Contemporaries of Raleigh and Queen Elizabeth I professed that the handsome, charming sailor was a favorite of the queen, thanks to his wit, manners, and usefulness to her. Raleigh's intense passion for the colonization project is likely to have swayed the queen in continuing to give permission for his expeditions, despite the continued failure of English colonies to persevere. To repay Raleigh for his services, Elizabeth awarded him a monopoly on the wine trade and named him captain of the Queen's Guard.

Raleigh sailed from England in 1584 to explore the western shores of America and to find the ideal place in which to plant his settlers. He found what he was looking for at Roanoke Island, located just offshore from modern-day North Carolina. Upon his return to England, he presented Queen Elizabeth I with his maps, data, and official plans, but she refused to give him the funding he needed to carry it out. The queen knew it was a high-risk venture and didn't dare invest the kingdom's gold; she did, however, allow Raleigh to solicit investments from private businessmen. Within a year, Raleigh collected sufficient funds for the expedition and sailed once more to Roanoke with 107 colonists.[67] They landed there in July of 1585 and named the colony "Virginia," in honor of the queen's popular moniker, "The Virgin Queen."[68]

---

[66] "Queen Elizabeth I: Colonizing America." *Royal Museums Greenwich.* Web.

[67] Ibid.

[68] Ibid.

The first colony at Virginia was abandoned after a spell of harsh weather and lack of supplies. Interest in the project was still high, however, and so, a second attempt was made in July of 1587.[69] This time, there were 150 colonists, including many families.[70] Things were hopeful from the outset, particularly given the good summer weather the colonists found upon arrival. Only a month after landing, the birth of Virginia Dare was recorded as the first English baby born on American soil.

Unfortunately, though it was still summer, the settlers had arrived too late to plant and harvest their crops. To tide them over, Virginia Governor John White went back to England to stock up on supplies. Once he came home, however, he found England on the edge of war with Spain. All the ships that had been intended to return to Virginia with food and other necessities were quickly recruited into the queen's navy. Consequently, the return voyage was postponed until 1590.[71]

War had been looming for many years between Spain and England for three primary reasons. First, Spain was fiercely loyal to the Catholic Church in Rome, while England had broken off completely with the pope. Secondly, Spain had laid claim to huge swathes of land in the New World and found huge quantities of pure gold there, which were regularly pirated by English vessels. Third, the ongoing Dutch Protestant rebellions against Spain were blatantly supported by England.

Two major battles were fought in 1587 and 1588: The Battle of Cadiz and the Battle of the Armada. These both saw England victorious, and a break in the violence meant that John White could set sail for America once more. When he finally did return, the

[69] Ibid.

[70] Ibid.

[71] Ibid.

colony had been abandoned, and the word "CROATOAN" was carved into a tree trunk. John White assumed the colonists had moved to Croatoan Island, but bad weather prevented him from following up on his theory. Furthermore, the war with Spain continued, and there was no time nor funding for further attempts at American settlement. In fact, there were no successful English settlements in the Americas until 1607, when the Virginia Company created the Jamestown settlement.[72]

Meanwhile, there were many adventurous sailors and merchants eager to cash in on all the valuable goods available to England in the opposite direction to America. India had its own wealth to offer, and so, one group in particular met formally on September 22nd, 1599, to commit to establishing its own Indian trading company with £30,133.[73] They also collected sailing ships for the venture, which more than doubled the cost of their project. On December 31st of that same year, Queen Elizabeth I granted a royal charter to "George, Earl of Cumberland, and 215 Knights, Aldermen, and Burgesses" under the name "Governor and Company of Merchants of London trading with the East Indies."[74]

The charter awarded the new company a complete monopoly on English trade with any countries east of Africa's Cape of Good Hope and west of the Strait of Magellan. Any other English merchants found conducting such trade were liable to have their goods and profits seized and distributed to the Crown and the East India Company. The original charter lasted for fifteen years and had strict, detailed rules about the governance of the company, which ultimately lay in the hands of the English courts.

---

[72] Ibid.

[73] Tietz, Tabea. "The Rise and Fall of the British East India Company." *SCIHI*. Web. 31 December 2013.

[74] ORR, Brian J. *Bones of Empire*. 2013.

Having sent expeditions to the west and east, Queen Elizabeth I cemented a prosperous future for her kingdom. By 1603, she had reigned for 44 years and had grown old. Soon after the establishment of the East India Company, the country's Virgin Queen died at the age of 69, ending not only the Elizabethan Era but the Tudor Dynasty.

Chapter Twelve – The House of Stuart

Elizabeth Tudor had never married or borne any children, which caused something of a panic in her advisors during her later years. She had also failed to name a successor until reportedly in her last hours of life—and this was merely a hand gesture interpreted by her secretary of state, Robert Cecil. Dying and unable to stand, Elizabeth indicated her forehead when Cecil asked if she wanted the Scottish king to succeed her. The secretary took this to mean she chose James VI, a member of the House of Stuart, to receive her crown.

Before Elizabeth died, she saw the very first voyage arranged by the East India Company, which was commanded by James Lancaster. Their business was not limited to just finding goods in India; the queen's appointed merchants also attacked and captured other ships they encountered during their voyages. Lancaster's ship, the *Red Dragon*, captured a Portuguese ship and annexed its own goods, using the funds to set up two manufacturing factories, one in Java and the other in the Maluku Islands, also known as the Spice Islands.

It was a successful start, but upon returning to England, the crew found that their benefactress, Queen Elizabeth, had died.

King James, now known as King James I after becoming the ruler of England and Ireland in addition to Scotland, decided to continue the patronage of the East India Company, thereby knighting Lancaster. The new king recognized that the company had secured England's future in the spice trade, particularly now that the war with Spain had finally come to an end. Furthermore, James was happy to continue on with many of his predecessor's policies concerning exploration and trade. While translating his own version of the Christian Bible, James found many opportunities to praise trade as the foundation of a strong community. In Genesis Ecclesiastes 34:21, the King James Bible reads, "These men are peaceable with us; therefore let them dwell in the land, and trade therein; for the land, behold, it is large enough for them; let us take their daughters to us for wives, and let us give them our daughters."

When trade was well established between India and England, a succession of Stuart monarchs promoted heavy emigration to the Americas to make up for having lagged behind the Spanish, French, and Dutch in that respect. Over the next century, England founded over ten colonies in the New World and regularly sent ships full of immigrants to live there. The movement of settlers eased the issues of poverty at home in England, which were due to the 16th-century rise in population. People with no money or property in England had no trouble being accepted on the migrant boats and being taken to colonies in Virginia and Maryland. Thousands of the migrants were brought to America to work in the tobacco fields of Chesapeake Bay. Many of the families who chose to make the long journey westward over the Atlantic Ocean ended up in Plymouth, Massachusetts Bay, New Haven, Connecticut, or Rhode Island Colonies, eager to practice their Puritan religion away from a country of more liberal Protestants.

While the English occupation of the New World grew significantly, the East India Company was also hard at work expanding the reach of England's merchants. Sailing ever farther from home, the *Clove*, under the umbrella of the East India Company, was the first English ship to reach Japan in June 1613.[75] Once the crew of the *Clove* stepped foot onto Japanese soil for the first time, the ship's captain, John Saris, met with Japan's leaders, retired shogun Tokugawa Ieyasu and his son, the current shogun, Tokugawa Hidetada, to exchange gifts. Saris gifted the shogun and his father with a telescope, a cup, and some English wool. In exchange, Hidetada presented Saris with two suits of armor. Ieyasu also presented Saris with ten gold-painted screens and a letter for King James I. The pair also happily gave the English captain an official vermilion sealed letter that granted Saris permission to live and work in Japan. It was a cordial and friendly meeting that began a warm long-distance friendship between the two countries.

The English set up a trading station in Hirado, located on the island of Kyushu, Japan's southernmost island, and discovered that Japan did not have a brewing industry. Saris' ship was well stocked with beer for the crew, as drinking was a common practice throughout Europe, so they offered it to their hosts. The Japanese thirst for beer proved to be quite insatiable, giving England and its competitor, Holland, another item to add to its cargo on future voyages to the Far East. Saris returned to London in December 1614, and King James was reportedly quite pleased with his gifts.

King James enjoyed a great deal of power as the king of Scotland, as there were fewer checks and balances imposed upon him as were used in England. Once he inherited Elizabeth I's throne and became James I of England in 1603, the monarch realized that ruling England would not be quite the same as he was accustomed to.[76] The king, being a peaceful man, did not see fit to try to reorganize the English political system to his own taste; he accepted that he was responsible to Parliament and must work in tandem with the

---

[75] "Timeline." *The East India Trading Company London.* Web.

[76] Doelman, James. *King James I and the Religious Culture of England.* 2000.

parliamentarians. James' reign did not suffer overmuch from controversy, though his personal debts and Catholic baptism were the sources of some dissension.

The same could not be said of the reign of James' heir, Charles I. Charles inherited the thrones of Scotland, England, and Ireland in 1625 after his father's death and began a tenuous rule over the kingdoms.[77] Charles, born in 1600, had been left behind in Scotland as a baby, even though other members of his family had moved to England, because his health was considered to be too delicate for such a long journey.[78] About a year after the rest of his family moved, young Charles took the trip and was given into the care of Sir Robert and Lady Carey. It was due to Lady Carey's influence that the young boy, who had trouble walking as well as speaking, was not forced into iron boots. He overcame his problems of walking of his own volition, but nevertheless, he was considered socially awkward due to his permanent Scottish accent and tendency to stutter.

Charles was truly religious and had been raised Protestant, as had his English counterparts. Generally a shy young man, he put a great deal of importance on the teachings of his father. Charles I believed, as had James I, that God had created him to be put on the thrones of the British Isles and rule over the people in their best interests. Because of that belief, Charles found it difficult to trust the English Parliament and often did what he could to side-step their advice. In avoiding these politicians, both in England and Scotland, he cultivated a lot of negativity.

Between the years of 1629 and 1640, Charles went as far as to completely dismiss Parliament, deciding instead to rule by royal decree. This period has been called both the "Personal Rule," and the

---

[77] Ashley, Maurice. "Charles I." *Encyclopedia Britannica*. Web.

[78] Ibid.

"Eleven Years' Tyranny."[79] Since he could no longer go to Parliament for financial support, Charles I grasped at outdated tax schemes to collect funds, such as ship money. These taxes were first levied from coastal towns and counties for maritime protection in wartime, starting centuries earlier. Specifically, ship money required such communities to provide the navy with ships or to pay the equivalent value in money. Though traditionally this tax only applied to maritime communities, Charles I insisted that it also be applied to inland regions. This, of course, proved to be quite unpopular with the people.

Charles' next great issue was that of religion. Though he personally was dedicated to Protestantism, his wife, Queen Henrietta Maria of France, was Roman Catholic. The Catholic queen made many Protestant English people nervous, but neither she nor Charles made a move to reinstate England as a papal state. Instead, the king was intent on the use of the *Book of Common Prayer* and following rituals. Though this may have appeased an earlier generation of English people, by Charles I's reign, a large portion of England identified as Puritan. The Puritans followed much of the same doctrine as the Protestants did; however, they wanted to remove the intricate rituals and decorations that were prominent in the Church of England. It was no coincidence that most parliamentarians had been Puritan when they were dismissed by the king.

In Scotland, the religious whims of King Charles I went over even more poorly than they had in England. Many Scottish people were Presbyterian, an offshoot of Protestantism, and they were not happy to be told by Charles I that they should be following the example of the Church of England. In fact, when the king attempted to impose his own prayer book in Scottish churches in 1637, a riot broke out in Edinburgh that signaled the readying of the people to lead their country into the Bishops' Wars.[80] The religious skirmish would soon

---

[79] Ibid.

[80] Ashley, Maurice. "Charles I." *Encyclopedia Britannica.* Web.

develop into a wholescale civil war that threatened the future of the royal House of Stuart, as well as the political bond between England and Scotland.

Chapter Thirteen – Civil War

King Charles I met with the first serious act of defiance against his reign in November of 1638 when Glasgow's General Assembly openly agreed to ignore the king's orders concerning the Church of Scotland. Unwilling to let such treason against his authority go unpunished, the king gathered an English army and set toward the Scottish border in 1639.[81] Unfortunately, the king's army lacked sufficient funding and training, which meant that diplomacy won out over violence. Charles agreed, via the treaty known as the Pacification of Berwick, to leave the Scots alone when it came to religion. This was the first, bloodless, Bishops' War.

The pacification treaty was of little use except in preventing immediate battle; authorities on both sides held different interpretations of the treaty and therefore were soon right back where they had started. Charles soon learned that the Scottish lords were communicating with their allies in France and took this to mean England's two ancient enemies were plotting war against him. Once more, the king decided to raise an army, but this time, he wanted it to be bigger, stronger, and better prepared than it had been the previous year. To raise money, Charles I had little choice but to

---

[81] "Bishops' Wars." *Encyclopedia Britannica.* Web.

assemble the English Parliament for the first time in eleven years in April of 1640.[82]

Once assembled, the English lords refused to speak to the king about fundraising and army-building until they first discussed what they believed should be their role in his government. Once these grievances had been tabled, Parliament made it clear that they did not support a war against Scotland. Seeing that he would get nowhere with the lords, Charles decided to go about things his own way once more, earning this brief respite from the Personal Rule the moniker the "Short Parliament." Determinedly, Charles raised an army again and marched on Scotland. Things did not go well for him; the Scottish forces not only kept the royal army from seizing any land in Scotland, but they also captured much of northern England for themselves. This was the second Bishops' War.

To further confound matters for King Charles I, rebels in Ireland organized their own revolution in October of 1641.[83] There were many reasons for the Irish uprising, including their desire to have the Roman Catholic Church reinstated as the ruling authority in their land. At the time, both Catholics and Protestants resided in Ireland in large numbers side by side, and the relations between the two groups had grown incredibly tense. Catholic rebels instigated violence against their Protestant neighbors, which resulted in the loss of thousands of lives. Historians believe that as many as 4,000 Irish Protestants were killed in the uprising, but in England, those numbers were greatly exaggerated, either out of fear and rumors or as political leverage to act against the Catholics.[84] Not all the rebels were resolved to kill their Protestant fellows, however, and instead focused their efforts on pillaging Protestant property and stealing

---

[82] Ibid.

[83] Ibid.

[84] *Ibid.*

anything of value. These offenses were paid back in kind by the persecuted Protestants.

With his kingdom in great peril, King Charles I called his government together yet another time to try to find a solution to the predicaments. In November of 1640, the English lords assembled again in what would be called the "Long Parliament."[85] The Long Parliament was incredibly quick and effective in securing its own existence. Within a year of its reinstatement, Parliament completely overhauled the English governing system and removed the king's counselors from positions of power. The government passed a law that required regular meetings and also made further dissolutions of Parliament illegal without the express consent of its members.

The king tried to keep his government in check, even moving to arrest five parliamentary lords in January of 1642, but his efforts failed.[86] The five men—John Pym, John Hampden, Denzil Holles, William Strode, and Sir Arthur Haselrig—were potentially involved in collusion with Scotland. Charles intended to try each for treason, but their peers refused to hand them over. The incident took place in the House of Commons, and the king sent guards there to arrest the men. Believing that the king was acting out of order, as it was against protocol for members of the monarchy to enter the parliamentary chambers or try to meddle in its affairs, the parliamentarians rudely shut their doors on the guards without handing over the wanted men or providing any information as to their whereabouts. Eventually, Charles himself came to the House and had no better luck retrieving information from his government. The men had clearly been prewarned of their impending danger and made an escape earlier in the day.

One of the parliamentarians who refused to comply with the king's demands was Oliver Cromwell, a wealthy Puritan from

---

[85] Ibid.

[86] "Charles I enters the House of Commons." *European Royal History*. Web. 2018.

Huntingdonshire. At the end of 1642, failure by both Parliament and the king to concede to the other's demands came to a violent breaking point. Both parties had already been amassing armies and funds, just in case they should have need, and across the countryside, noble families scrambled to provide secure housing for members of one side or the other. They also contributed soldiers, weapons, ammunition, and money to the side of their choice.

Oliver Cromwell and many of his allies in Parliament had been greatly influenced by Thomas Beard, a Puritanical clergyman and author of *The Theatre of Gods Judgements*. Beard's book, which portrayed the Catholic pope as the anti-Christ, was a religious treatise that convinced many English people, including Oliver Cromwell, that serious changes were needed in contemporary religions. Cromwell undoubtedly became more anti-Catholic after studying with Beard, though his family's Protestant teachings had already predisposed him to do so. Though the Church of England had been created as an alternative to Catholicism, Beard's and Cromwell's brand of Protestantism went a great deal further. Calling themselves Puritans, supporters of Beard's ideas belonged to a religious order in which Catholicism was considered so blasphemous that any decoration or festivity that could be likened to a Catholic tradition was banned.

Puritanical theory was largely behind Cromwell's decision to fight against the monarchy, and they helped the war effort by blocking a shipment of silver meant for the king and gathering soldiers from Cambridgeshire. After a series of military engagements against the king's army, Cromwell became a military commander in the rebel army. As the battles continued, Parliament was cleared of all men unwilling to try King Charles for treason, leaving behind a small selection known as the Rump Parliament. The Rump Parliament eventually proved less cooperative than the rebels had hoped, and on

April 20th, 1653, Oliver Cromwell brought an army to the Houses of Parliament to clear them all out.[87]

He burst in, just as the king had done a year earlier, and said the following:

> It is high time for me to put an end to your sitting in this place, which you have dishonored by your contempt of all virtue, and defiled by your practice of every vice; ye are a factious crew, and enemies to all good government; ye are a pack of mercenary wretches, and would like Esau sell your country for a mess of pottage, and like Judas betray your God for a few pieces of money.
>
> Is there a single virtue now remaining amongst you? Is there one vice you do not possess? Ye have no more religion than my horse; gold is your God; which of you have not barter'd your conscience for bribes? Is there a man amongst you that has the least care for the good of the Commonwealth?
>
> Ye sordid prostitutes have you not defil'd this sacred place, and turn'd the Lord's temple into a den of thieves, by your immoral principles and wicked practices? Ye are grown intolerably odious to the whole nation; you were deputed here by the people to get grievances redress'd, are yourselves gone! So! Take away that shining bauble there, and lock up the doors.
>
> In the name of God, go![88]

In place of the Rump Parliament, Cromwell installed a Nominated Assembly in July 1653, which was also known as the Barebones Parliament.[89] The Nominated Assembly members numbered 144,

---

[87] "Civil War." *UK Parliament Website.* Web.

[88] "Oliver Cromwell Speech – Dissolution of The Long Parliament 1653." *The Britpolitics Treasury.* Web.

[89] "Civil War." *UK Parliament Website.* Web.

---

and each was selected by rebel army officers, who looked for those who were the most godly and committed to religious reform. However, even the Nominated Assembly participated in discussions and measures for social reform that displeased Cromwell and his supporters. Of particular concern was the fact that the parliamentarians were obviously quite leery of the army and were fearful of being forced to instate specific legislation by threat of violence.

Just a few months later, on the morning of December 12th, 1653, a faction of the rebel army led by General John Lambert swept into Parliament and voted once more to have the whole group dissolved.[90] It all took place while many members of the assembly were out at a prayer meeting. Lambert, like everyone involved, had grown tired of the succession of disappointing parliamentary bodies, and he had come up with a better idea. He wrote his plan down as the "Instrument of Government" and stated that the best form of government with which to go forward must consist of one ruler and his parliament. It was like a constitutional monarchy, except that King Charles would not be the ruler; that privilege was awarded to Oliver Cromwell. On December 16th,1653, Oliver Cromwell was officially named Lord Protector of the Realm.[91]

---

[90] Ibid.

[91] Ibid.

Chapter Fourteen – The Protectorate

Cromwell appointed his own government and called it the Council of State. His first order of business was to arrest King Charles and have him tried in court for treason against England. While the war continued between the royalist army and that of Cromwell, the deposed king was hidden in southern England under the protection of his own guards. In 1644, the Oxford Parliament was assembled to support the king, but it faltered the next year.[92] Charles rode into battle with his army several times as the civil war dragged on, but by that time, the parliamentary forces were gaining ground on the royalists. Support for Cromwell's Protectorate rule was widespread, and the Lord Protector's army was enthusiastic in defending his authority. The fighting became so chaotic that Charles was forced to entrust his life in the hands of the Scottish army, who took him north to Newcastle upon Tyne. The Scots negotiated with Cromwell's government for nine long months before finally coming to an agreement: They would hand Charles over to the English Parliament in exchange for £100,000 upon delivery and more money afterward

---

[92] Gregg, Pauline. *King Charles I*. 1981.

in installments.[93] The Scottish army delivered Charles to the parliamentary commissioners in January of 1647.[94]

Cromwell sent the recaptured prisoner to Holdenby House in Northamptonshire. Outside, divisions appeared among the anti-royalist army, which split into one group of those loyal to Cromwell, known as the Parliamentarians, and another called the New Model Army. The New Model Army wanted more control in government administration, while the Parliamentarians preferred to establish the Church of England as a Puritanical Presbyterian body, and then step down and give up their authority. Charles fully realized that the factious state of his opponent's army could be very beneficial to him, so he therefore went willingly with the New Model Army when it arrived at Holdenby House to take him into its own custody. Charles enjoyed a great deal of authority with the New Model Army, and when he encouraged his new captors to take him to Hampton Court, they obliged.

Charles managed once more to flee his lavish prison, but he wrongfully trusted Colonel Robert Hammond, the parliamentary governor of the Isle of Wight, and ended up back in custody soon afterward. This time, he was held at Carisbrooke Castle on the Isle of Wight. Charles was treated well and given every opportunity to repent of what his opponent deemed to be the sin of treason, but Charles refused to do so. Instead of seeking diplomacy, Charles simply refused to recognize the authority of Lord Protector Cromwell or to accept that England's ancient monarchy had been defeated. Instead, he tried ceaselessly to negotiate with outside parties who might secure his release. One of those parties was the Scottish government, whom he decided to trust despite the Scottish army's having turned him over to the English Parliament less than one year prior. Nevertheless, on December 26th, 1647, Charles

---

[93] Ibid.

[94] Ibid.

signed a secret treaty with Scotland.[95] The terms were that Scotland must invade England on behalf of the deposed king and restore him to the crown; in return, Charles would convert the Church of England to Presbyterianism.

The Scottish did what they promised, and the royalist army within England rose up again to help them. The fighting began in May of the next year, but the royalists and Scots were thoroughly beaten by August. Charles' only hope was to establish some diplomacy between himself and the Parliamentarians, and so, both parties looked toward a meeting. The acting English Parliament voted on whether to meet with the king, and the "yes" votes outnumbered the "no" votes 129 to 83.[96] Cromwell and his loyal army would do no such thing, however, arguing that there was no sense in debating with a known tyrant. A series of arrests were made on any known royalist sympathizers, including many members of Parliament, which effectively left another scant Rump Parliament whose ideals mimicked those of Cromwell.

In January 1649, the Rump Parliament indicted Charles I for treason, but it had difficulty carrying out any sort of trial since England's three acting chief justices argued that there was no law under which a monarch could be tried in court. Defiantly, Parliament stated that it was capable of creating laws without the need for collaboration with any other legislative group and thereby passed a legal bill to create an entirely new court system just for the king's trial. The High Court, which was created for this purpose, consisted of 135 members, but half of these stayed away from the proceedings either voluntarily or by coercion from Cromwell since they were uncomfortable with sitting in judgment over the king.[97]

---

[95] Cust, Richard. *Charles I: A Political Life*. 2005.

[96] Coward, Barry. *The Stuart Age* (Third edition). 2003.

[97] Gregg, Pauline. *King Charles I*. 1981.

At the official trial, Charles I was accused of treason against his country by having used his power to pursue projects in his own interest rather than acting for the good of his country. The High Court, therefore, held Charles responsible for all the crimes and travesties that had passed during the civil war, including some 300,000 deaths.[98] For his part, Charles refused to give any plea and repeatedly asked his prosecutors by whose authority they had brought him there—since, as king, he answered to no higher authority except that of God. Charles was found guilty of treason on January 26th, 1649, and was sentenced to death.[99] He was beheaded in Whitehall four days later.[100]

Following the king's death, Oliver Cromwell established the Commonwealth of England. The Rump Parliament, of which Cromwell himself was a member, continued on alongside a small Council of State. As the head of the Council of State and leader of the army, Cromwell's own power remained in place. Most royalists fled to Ireland and made an alliance with Irish Catholics after the death of Charles I, and Cromwell set out later that same year to meet them in battle. His campaign was long-winded but ultimately successful, having gained English authority in each critical Irish city. As soon as the Irish campaign had met its end, however, Cromwell faced fresh defiance from the Scots, who had named Charles Stuart II—the son of the late Charles I—the king of Scotland. After sending his army to Scotland to successfully wrestle back control, Cromwell was named Lord Protector for life in a new version of the "Instrument of Government," which served as England's constitution.

The leader of the Commonwealth of England died in 1658 from what is believed to have been a combination of malaria and

---

[98] Carlton, Charles. *Charles I: The Personal Monarch* (Second edition). 1995.

[99] "The Execution of Charles I." *Historic Royal Palaces.* Web.

[100] "The Execution of Charles I." *Historic Royal Palaces.* Web.

infection.[101] Cromwell's son Richard inherited his position as Lord Protector, but he lacked his father's military genius, network of loyal parliamentarians, and army personnel. By May of 1659, Richard Cromwell stepped down as Lord Protector, and another Long Parliament was reinstated.[102] Parliament arranged to have Charles II take up his post as the king of England, Ireland, and Scotland, and thus, the House of Stuart was established back on the throne in 1660.

---

[101] *McMains, H.F. The Death of Oliver Cromwell. 2015.*

[102] "Richard Cromwell, English Statesman." *Encyclopedia Britannica.* Web.

Chapter Fifteen – The Glorious Revolution

On February 6th, 1685, James II (known as James VII in Scotland) inherited the thrones of England and Ireland in addition to the throne of Scotland he already occupied. His succession was largely supported by the concept of divine law and birth in all three nations, but James' popularity would not last long. He was very open-minded about the practice of non-conformist religions, which in England generally meant Roman Catholicism or splinter Protestant groups. Two years into his reign, James II issued the Declaration of Indulgence, which put a stop to penalties that had been inflicted on the king's subjects for not following the doctrine of the Church of England or the Church of Scotland. After drafting the document himself in April 1687, the king required all churches in his realm to read it on two consecutive Sundays.

James II was a practicing Catholic, and as such, he was unwilling to conform to Anglicanism as others had done before him. Instead, he envisioned a realm in which there was widespread religious tolerance for Catholicism and all the branches of Christianity. Unfortunately, his government and the people of his kingdoms heartily disagreed with such an idea, as a healthy fear of Catholic tradition had been instilled in them over the years. There was a vicious pushback against the Declaration of Indulgence that ultimately led to the downfall of the king himself.

Determined to remain an Anglican country, the people of England favored a religious movement toward minimalism and humility. They believed that Catholic practices were gaudy, luxurious, and did not keep with obeying God's will. The anti-Catholic sentiment ran so deep that England's Archbishop of Canterbury, William Sancroft, and six other bishops wrote a petition against it. They were tried with seditious libel but eventually let go. Soon afterward, James II and Queen Mary of Modena had a son, further aggravating the monarch's detractors. With a son and male heir in place, the Catholic king and queen were perfectly positioned to set up a new religious regime. Their elder daughter, Mary, stood next in line after her brother, and despite the fears of the English parliamentarians and clergy, both children were raised Anglican.

Desperate for a strong anti-Catholic ruler, several English politicians from both the Whig and Tory Parties formed a plan with the help of a bishop. These men wrote directly to William Hendrik, a Dutch cousin of the English royal family whose title was Prince of Orange, asking for his help. Best known as William of Orange, the Dutch prince was very popular, and what's more, he was a staunch Protestant and had married James II's oldest daughter Mary in 1677.[103] Because of his heritage, William of Orange stood fourth in line to the English throne, and his wife was second.

Each petitioner signed his name on the invitation, revealing themselves to be Charles Talbot, Earl of Shrewsbury; William Cavendish, Earl of Devonshire; Thomas Osborne, Earl of Danby; Richard, Viscount Lumley; Henry Compton, Bishop of London; Edward Russell; and Henry Sydney.

Their invitation read:

---

[103] "William III." *Encyclopedia Britannica.* Web.

...The people are so generally dissatisfied with the present conduct of the government in relation to their religion, liberties and properties (all which have been greatly invaded), and they are in such expectation of their prospects being daily worse, that Your Highness may be assured there are nineteen parts of twenty of the people throughout the kingdom who are desirous of a change and who, we believe, would willingly contribute to it, if they had such a protection to countenance their rising as would secure them from being destroyed before they could get to be in a posture to defend themselves...

These considerations make us of the opinion that this is a season in which we may more probably contribute to our own safeties than hereafter (although we must own to Your Highness there are some judgments differing from ours in this particular), insomuch that if the circumstances stand so with Your Highness that you believe you can get here time enough, in a condition to give assistances this year sufficient for a relief under these circumstances which have been now represented, we who subscribe this will not fail to attend Your Highness upon your landing and to do all that lies in our power to prepare others to be in as much readiness as such an action is capable of, where there is so much danger in communicating an affair of such a nature till it be near the time of its being made public.[104]

The anti-Catholic plotters wrote pleadingly to William many times, inviting him to join their cause and help resolve the grievances of the people. William corresponded with them for about a year before seeing an opportunity to provide his services and also use that relationship to benefit peace negotiations with other European nations. France, Italy, and the Netherlands had been upon the edge of war for many years at that point, though by 1688, they had begun to

---

[104] Browning, Andrew (editor). *English Historical Documents, 1660-1714*. 1953.

form a peaceful alliance in favor of stopping all attacks. William knew that the chances for a successful peace in Europe would be greatly increased if England lent its support, and it was largely for that reason that he decided to travel to England. He went with 500 ships and 14,000 fighting men.[105]

William of Orange landed at Tor Bay in Brixham on November 5th, 1688, intent on taking London.[106] His movements were neither violent nor rapid; the prince made his way to the capital city at a casual pace, gauging the support for his cause and learning how the English truly felt about their king. Finding the situation to be much as it was described to him in the letters, William's journey to London was a confident one. Even John Churchill, James II's general, and the king's daughter, Anne, had joined the supportive crowd in favor of William. Before the Dutch prince even made it to London, James II had abandoned his castle and fled to France.

The government of England decided officially that James II's flight from London should be documented as a case of abdication. William was crowned in London on April 21st, 1689, as was his queen, Mary II, daughter of James II.[107] Theirs was a constitutional monarchy that was fully supportive of the Church of England. Afterward, the whole affair was called the Glorious Revolution, in which not a drop of blood had been spilled. The same could not be said of Scotland and Ireland, whose people fought against the regime change. Bloodshed followed, but later that same year, Scotland offered William III the crown, and Ireland was reconquered.

The new king and queen ruled jointly until Mary's death in 1694; William lived for about ten more years, dying in 1702.

---

[105] "William III, Prince of Orange, Arriving at Brixham." *Royal Collection Trust.* Web.

[106] "Glorious Revolution." *Encyclopedia Britannica.* Web.

[107] "William III, Prince of Orange, Arriving at Brixham." *Royal Collection Trust.* Web.

Chapter Sixteen – The Scientific Revolution

Just as long-held political theories were being put into practice, so, too, were an astonishing number of ideas concerning the systems that governed the way the world and universe functioned. With extreme vigor, England's scientists were putting ancient Greek theories to the test and were often making discoveries that would have confounded their long-dead predecessors. Astronomy was extremely popular among the highly educated of the kingdom, and in particular, many astronomers strove to prove or disprove the theory posited by Polish scientist Nicolaus Copernicus that the Earth revolved around the Sun.

On November 28th, 1660, the Royal Society of London was founded by a group of Englishmen who wanted to promote scientific experimentation.[108] The founders of the Society included the mathematician, scientist, and architect responsible for Saint Paul's Cathedral, Christopher Wren; chemist and inventor Robert Boyle; and physician, scientist, and philosopher William Petty. Excited to form a formal membership of learned, scientific thinkers, the

---

[108] "History of the Royal Society." *Royal Society.* Web.

Society's founders dedicated themselves to the development of scientific and mathematical learning. They set about making introductions to noted experimentalists of the day and soon gained a royal charter from King Charles II.

Robert Boyle designed most of the experiments conducted by the members of the Society, including his own series of trials concerning gas volumes and pressure. Through a great deal of experimentation, Boyle discovered that the volume of a gas decreases as its pressure increases and that the volume increases with decreased pressure. This relationship would come to be known as Boyle's law.[109] This understanding helped Boyle further theorize that gas was comprised of many tiny particles with spaces between them that could be compressed under pressure. His belief that perhaps matter was made of small pieces was groundbreaking, and only a few other scientists would corroborate his theory in the next century.

From 1703 to 1727, the president of the Royal Society was Sir Isaac Newton, the world-famous physicist and mathematician. Newton had his start in the sciences from a young age, and one of his most important discoveries had its roots in an event that occurred during his college years. During a particularly bad year of the plague, Newton and his fellow students were sent home for eighteen months, and studies were suspended. While at home, Isaac Newton spent his time studying and wondering about the mysteries of the universe. One day, while sitting in his garden, he saw an apple fall from a nearby tree and strike the ground. The movement of the apple fascinated Newton, who was inspired to work out the physical mechanics of a universe in which objects were obliged to fall to the ground. It was the beginning of a lifelong obsession with gravity and physical motion—as well as the start of a new field of science, physics.

---

[109] "Boyle's Law." *Science History Institute*. Web. 1 December 2017.

Newton was the pride of the Society for a generation, though he had his share of critics within the membership. While a member, Newton completed his great work, PHILOSOPHIÆ NATURALIS PRINCIPIA MATHEMATICA (MATHEMATICAL PRINCIPLES OF NATURAL PHILOSOPHY), AND PUBLISHED IT IN 1687. PRINCIPIA laid out the mathematics behind the mechanical forces of the universe and introduced the world to the theory of gravity. Newton started by studying the works of Johannes Kepler, a German astronomer who had inferred several laws of planetary motion from his astronomical observations. Using his own observations of the trajectories of comets, tides, and the movements of the stars, the Sun, and the Moon, Newton formulated his own laws of motion. His work helped the scientific community finally accept—for the most part—the heliocentric model of the universe as proposed by Copernicus and other scientists who had been demonized by religious groups.

The Royal Society of London flourished, acting as a haven for English scientists and a friendly place for international visitors to exhibit their work. The Society endured into the 19th century and is still around today, albeit it on a smaller scale. Just as its founders had intended, it inspired a great desire in England's citizens to learn more about modern science. One such person was Mary Somerville, an unusual addition to the Society's roster due to her sex. Though the Society believed only men should be admitted, they were interested in Mary's work with ultraviolet light. She was the first woman whose work—*The Magnetic Properties of the Violet Rays of the Solar Spectrum*—was granted an audience with the Society members. Published in 1826, the work attempted to prove that ultraviolet light did indeed have magnetic properties that could be passed onto metal objects. Mary's husband, however, was invited to read the report instead of her.

Though the Royal Society of London enjoyed the membership of many intelligent scientists, it remained a men-only space until 1945. The men and many unnamed or forgotten women of the Scientific Revolution in England contributed a huge amount of work and data to the world, which would continue to be built upon more with each successive generation.

Chapter Seventeen – Great Britain Emerges

Though England and Scotland had shared a monarch since 1603, they were not technically united under the law. Technically, there could still be different monarchs ruling each kingdom if the circumstances demanded it, but King James I had been adamant in referring to his realms as Great Britain. James even brought a proposal to Parliament upon his coronation to formally unite the two countries, but it was not very popular. Nevertheless, the king persevered for several years to try to implement a unified Church of Scotland and England alongside a unified state of Great Britain. In 1604, he commissioned the creation of a new flag that combined England's red cross on white with Scotland's blue X on white. It was called the Union Jack, "Jack" being a shortened version of "Jacobus," the Latin version of James.[110] Ultimately, the plan was unsuccessful, and James blamed its failure on the English.

The official Union of the Crowns did eventually take place, though, but not until 1707. [111] There were many hurdles for the proponents

---

[110] "Union of the Crowns." *Parliament.* Web.

[111] "Union of the Crowns." *Parliament.* Web.

of a union to overcome before the idea truly took hold, including, of course, the English Civil War and the subsequent reinstitution of the Stuart monarchy under King Charles II. Over the following decades, the topic moved in and out of Parliament, both in England and Scotland, gaining support and waning again in cycles. Many parliamentarians and members of the clergy on both sides could not see why they would benefit from such an arrangement, and thus, it was eternally dismissed.

This began to change following the Glorious Revolution of 1688. [112] The next year, a convention was held in Edinburgh with several Scottish bishops openly supporting a renewal of the idea of a union. By this time, the two kingdoms were ruled under King William III and Queen Mary II, with William having taken over the crown from his unpopular Catholic cousin James II. As a Protestant who had helped England fight against France, William and his queen were very popular in both Scotland and England. The monarchs supported a union, but despite their good reputation, they faced overwhelming criticism on the subject from Scottish Presbyterians and the English Parliament.

Just a few scant years afterward, however, Scotland suffered a very damaging economic downturn that likely convinced many of its clergy and politicians to change their minds about forming a union. It was called the Seven Ill Years, during which Scotland's financial and economic crisis resulted in its developing closer, more urgent ties with England. Beginning around 1690, Scotland experienced seven years of drought, bad weather, and food shortages that were so severe they caused a sharp rise in deaths from starvation. [113] Much of Europe experienced the same type of situation, but it was particularly bad in Scotland. When temperatures much lower than normal killed the oatmeal crops of Scottish farmers in 1693, their

---

[112] "National Covenant." *Encyclopedia Britannica*. Web.

[113] "The Seven Ill Years." *Ancestry*. Web.

primary food source was lost for years afterward. To prevent starvation, the Scots were forced to eat whatever they could find, including grass and rotting meat. Two more extreme crop failures occurred before the turn of the century.

There was another reason for Scotland's trouble that decade: The Company of Scotland Trading to Africa and the Indies. This new company was created by the Scottish Parliament in 1695 for the purpose of establishing a Scottish trading monopoly.[114] It was a fundamental goal of the Company of Scotland to build a colony in Panama, whereby their merchant ships could better reach the Americas and Asia. Almost all of the funding for the company's project came from Scottish investors. Unfortunately, the colonization of Panama was a disaster due to climatic, health, and political reasons; the settlers found themselves battling against Spanish sailors who did not want to see rival European nations in the Americas. The remaining colonists left, never to return, in 1700, with the company having lost its investors more than £150,000.[115]

The combined devastation wrought upon Scotland by such a huge financial loss and unstable agriculture is considered to be some of the most important factors behind Scotland's decision to pursue a union with England. By 1702, Queen Anne—sister to William III's wife, Mary II—had ascended to the throne of the kingdoms of England, Scotland, and Ireland.[116] Under her request, the Parliaments of England and Scotland agreed to meet once more to try to come to a satisfactory union deal.

For the negotiations, both countries selected 31 commissioners to operate on their behalf. Though most Scottish commissioners were in favor of a union, a much larger majority of the Scottish citizens

---

[114] "Company of Scotland Trading to Africa and the Indies." *RBS*. Web. 2017.

[115] Devine, Tom M. *Recovering Scotland's Slavery Past*. 2015.

[116] "Anne." *Encyclopedia Britannica*. Web.

were firmly against such a thing. On the English side, most of the appointed commissioners were also in favor of unity. The formal negotiations took place in London in 1706, between April 16th and July 22nd.[117] There were many concerns tabled during that week, including Scotland's fear that a union would require them to change their religion and England's fear that Scotland would try to appoint a new monarch to its own throne. To quell these primary concerns, the Scots agreed on a successor to Queen Anne, and the English agreed to minimal organizational changes to the Church of Scotland. The Scots were also promised direct access to England's colonial markets.

Both sides signed the legislation into an official treaty on January 16th, 1707. It passed with 110 votes to 69.[118] Daniel Defoe, an eminent English political pamphleteer who would later write the novel *Robinson Crusoe*, published the following account of the proceedings:

> Before I enter upon the Proceedings in the Reign of Queen ANNE, towards a General Union of these Kingdoms, it is absolutely necessary to the right Understanding of Things, to take a short View of the Posture of Publick Affairs in the respective Kingdoms, and what it was that rendered the Union so absolutely Necessary at the Time, that to all Considering People, who made any tolerable Judgement of Things, there was no other way left, to prevent the most Bloody War that ever had been between the two Nations...
>
> Thus, on both Sides, the case stood between the nations, a Pen and Ink War made a daily Noise in either Kingdom, and this served to Exasperate the People in such a manner, one

---

[117] Simpson, Robert. *The History of Scotland.* 1846.

[118] Campsie, Alison. "On this day 1707: Treaty of Union signed by Scottish Parliament." *The Scotsman.* 16 January 2019.

against another, that never have two Nations Run upon one another in such a manner, and come off without Blows.[119]

Thus, the United Kingdom was born, which included the countries of England, Scotland, Ireland, and Wales. But the British Empire, whose holdings included territories in the Americas, Asia, and Africa, was only going to grow in size and power in the following years. The British Empire did lose its strongest holding in the Americas when the American colonists rebelled against British rule in 1776, but Queen Victoria would help steer the empire back on a path toward domination when it came to the territories Britain held in India.

[119] Defoe, Daniel. *The History of the Union of Great Britain.* 1709.

Chapter Eighteen – The Victorian Era

The Victorian Era went hand in hand with the Industrial Revolution, and as such, it was a booming, influential, and unforgettable period in the history of England and the world. At its helm was Queen Victoria, yet another unlikely candidate for the throne of England. She was 18 years old at the time of her coronation in 1837, and her government ruled over Great Britain, Canada, Australia, India, New Zealand, and parts of Africa.

A significant factor in the changing economy and social fabric of Victorian-era Britain is the population explosion. When Victoria was first made queen, there were about 13.9 million Britons, and by the end of her reign, there were an estimated 32.5 million.[120] This marked increase is most likely due to improvements in medical science, sanitation, and welfare. The country's mortality rate fell, and simultaneously, its birth rate rose. The higher the population rose, the larger the nation's labor force became, and the easier it was for capitalism to take hold.

---

[120] Hughes, Trisha. *Virgin to Victoria.* 2018.

Capitalism went hand in hand with the Industrial Revolution, for which Britain lay the foundations by way of factories, fuel innovations, and pure inventiveness. Industrialization took place rapidly thanks to technological changes that allowed for the intensive manufacturing of valuable products like textiles, tools, clothing, and dishware. These changes involved the use of new types of materials such as steel, iron, coal, gas, and oil. The latter items were used as fuel in combustion engines that could power machines like the spinning jenny and the power loom. Machines, plentiful workers, and a stable fuel source could be combined into a productive factory business, and sales of items produced at such a factory could make owners rich.

Victoria's realm was the richest in Europe, as well as the first to industrialize on a large scale. However, while capitalists and the aristocracy brought in more money than ever before, the burden of Britain's poor grew worse. Jobs in factories were plentiful, but they also required long work hours, no vacation time, pitiful wages, and dangerous working conditions. Factory workers could barely provide for their families—if at all—and all the while, Britain's economy boomed off their underpaid labor. As for the people who couldn't find work at all, they were ordered to report to their local workhouse to perform factory labor in exchange for a space to sleep and two or three meals a day.

As difficult as it was for the queen's government to keep up with all the changes Britain was experiencing, doctors and medical scientists were taking great leaps forward. Medical treatments were advancing thanks to a better understanding of human anatomy, and the realm's many physicians were trained at the Royal College of Surgeons in London, the Glasgow Medical School, or Dublin's Catholic University School. As was the case at the Royal Society of London, only male students were admitted to these colleges, where the study of human cadavers was central to obtaining one's degree.

Students packed the university lecture halls to watch professional physicians perform autopsies on bodies in varied states of decay.

Such lessons were vital to training doctors and also for continuing to grow the field of medicine via detailed illustrations of the insides of these corpses. The Murder Act of 1751 legislated that no convicted murderer could be buried with other British citizens, so, therefore, they were given to schools; however, demand was still higher than supply. [121] In Edinburgh, a pair of men named William Burke and William Hare started a business of killing their lodgers and exchanging the fresh corpses for money to an Edinburgh medical doctor. Though murders like these were rare, many people did dig up bodies straight from the graveyard to sell them to medical universities.

The Victorians were obsessed with modernity and invention, but they were also sticklers when it came to church doctrine. All the same, it was a time when religion was mixed liberally with a few doses of superstition and spirituality. Séances and séance photography proved to be exceedingly popular in many Victorian circles, as thousands of British men and women attempted to make contact with the world of the dead. Victorian mediums were famous for conducting such boundary-crossing events in the parlors of their patrons, and they invited in spirits who evidently rocked tables, spewed ectoplasm, or even embodied a guest. The queen herself was rumored to have contacted a psychic medium to help her communicate with her deceased husband, Prince Albert, but no such proof has been found.

In 1858, Prime Minister Henry John Temple, better known as Lord Palmerston, passed the Government of India Act, which would dissolve the East India Company, placing its holdings under the British Crown. India had a long-standing relationship with Britain that dated back to the turn of the 17th century when the East India Trading Company established trading posts on Indian land. The trading company proved extremely successful, eventually buying up

---

[121] "The National Archives Education Service, Body Snatchers." *The National Archives.* Web.

a great deal of land and then simply taking it by force. As such, this act would have included the government of India, but before it could be passed, Lord Palmerston was forced to resign as prime minister, although a bill similar to the one Lord Palmerston proposed was passed that same year.[122] However, it wasn't until 1876, after Benjamin Disraeli had been returned to the office of prime minister, that Victoria earned the title "Empress of India." Although the Government of India Act had passed almost two decades before, it was the Royal Titles Act of 1876 that made the title official. The Government of India Act made India a more formal part of Great Britain, much in the way that Canada was. This was seen by many—both in India and Britain—as a positive move that would lead to more functional political systems. The organization of the country's government did change, and although more Indians were allowed positions of local power, they were generally kept out of the major ruling council.

Queen Victoria's reign was unlike any other in English history, thanks to an unprecedented series of inventions, discoveries, business projects, financial strategies, political gains, and social experimentation. Victoria herself was called the "Grandmother of Europe," thanks to the fact that her nine children married into other royal families on the continent, connecting a much larger community to England than ever before. By the time Victoria died in 1902, her people had started to grasp germ theory, mapped the human anatomy, invented machines capable of doing the work of many humans, and had even begun writing the first forms of science fiction.

---

[122] "India, Government of India Act, 1858." *Encyclopedia Britannica.* Web.

Chapter Nineteen – World War I

World War I, also known as the Great War, was the first large-scale military engagement between nations across the entire span of Europe using modern weapons. Even before heavy fire began throughout the continent, the Great War was underway in the guise of extremely delicate politics. The premise for the war was initially quite regional and was based on the assassination of Austria-Hungary's Archduke Franz Ferdinand and his wife, Sophie, by a Serbian rebel named Gavrilo Princip on June 28th, 1914. The archduke and heir to the throne of his country had been visiting Bosnia at the time of his murder, a nation in which there was great political upheaval following its annexation from Turkey into Austria-Hungary. The nation of Serbia had experienced the same treatment.

After the assassination, the Austria-Hungarian government blamed the Serbian government for the deaths of Franz Ferdinand and his wife, Duchess Sophie of Hohenberg. They declared war on Serbia on July 28th, 1914.[123] While Russia was allied with Serbia, Germany's Kaiser Wilhelm II did not believe Russia would actually get involved in the conflict and, therefore, boldly promised to provide support to Austria-Hungary. Russia, however, under the leadership

---

[123] "Austria-Hungary declares war on Serbia." *History.* Web. 2019.

of Tsar Nicolas II, did indeed decide to mobilize, calling on France to join them.

Great Britain was beholden to protect France and Belgium because of its own alliance treaties, and the German administration knew this; the latter tried to persuade Britain to forego its treaties and either join their cause or let Germany do as it pleased without consequences. In fact, it was in the Kaiser's best interests that Great Britain stay out of the coming war entirely, just as he had mistakenly expected from Russia.

It was Kaiser Wilhelm II's administration that was largely responsible for the development of WWI, due to his aggressive response to Russia stepping in to defend Serbia. On August 1st, 1914, Germany declared war on Russia.[124] On August 3rd, it declared war on France—and all of this was in the guise of defending Austria-Hungary, which had made no such declarations.[125] British Foreign Secretary Sir Edward Grey demanded that the troops be removed from Belgium; Germany ignored him. The Kaiser's hope was that in fighting a victorious war on the side of Austria-Hungary, Germany would be granted a large share of the spoils of war, particularly in terms of land.

On August 4th, Prime Minister Herbert Henry Asquith, better known as H.H. Asquith, recommended to King George V of Great Britain that they should declare war.[126] The basic reasons for Britain's declaration of war centered on giving support to France and preventing the Liberal Party from breaking apart, which was the party H.H. Asquith belonged to. In the British government, powerful Liberals threatened to resign if the government did not agree to send war aid to France, meaning that a solution must be found in order to

---

[124] "World War One Timeline." *History on the Net.* Web. 2019.

[125] Ibid.

[126] Bentley B. Gilbert. "Pacifist to interventionist: David Lloyd George in 1911 and 1914. Was Belgium an issue?" *Historical Journal.* 1985.

keep the Parliament functioning. The request was ironic, given the Liberals' strong anti-war faction; however, they argued that they had existing alliances that held them accountable for providing support to their French allies in times of war.[127] Furthermore, the government recognized that Belgium's ports were near the British shores, and therefore, German control of Belgium was a serious threat to Great Britain. King George V declared war on Germany within the space of just a few hours after the Germans occupied Belgium.

The United Kingdom had an overwhelmingly large empire at the time, which it was careful to maintain and protect. Furthermore, Britain did not want to see any other European superpower emerge, before or after the war. With this in mind, the government set about putting together a plan to both provide aid to its allies and maintain its own reputation as the economic powerhouse of Europe. That plan relied heavily on Britain's main source of wealth at the time, which was India. India was not only useful in terms of the tea trade, but it was also a huge resource in terms of manpower. Upon deciding to enter the Great War, both King George V and his government knew very well that India would have to provide vast numbers of soldiers for the war effort.

As it had been for centuries, Britain's greatest military resource was its navy. The Royal Navy had protected the British Isles from European attacks as far back as the 16th century, and it had spectacularly held off the Spanish Armada many times during the reign of Queen Elizabeth I. Having developed and depended on great warships for much of its history, Britain once more put its trust into the ability of its fighting men to protect the coastline and meet its enemies in battle on the sea.

The first major battle of the Great War took place that same month after the Russian army marched into Germany. It was difficult for

---

[127] Ibid.

the Russians to get supplies through to their people because of the variations in the railroad gauge between Russia and Prussia, but the tsar was determined to fight to victory following an embarrassing loss of his earlier war with Japan. On the other side, the Germans used their railway system to surround the Russian 2nd Army at Tannenberg, which is now a part of Poland. The ensuing battle resulted in a massive defeat for the Russians, who saw 125,000 soldiers taken prisoner by the Germans.[128]

Japan also declared war on Germany in August, in accordance with an alliance treaty it had signed with Great Britain in 1902.[129] The Ottoman Empire (modern-day Turkey) entered the war on the side of Austria-Hungary and Germany, after which point Russia officially declared war on the Ottoman Empire. In Britain, the government hoped that everything would be finished by Christmastime, but they were very much mistaken. Though the Russians had lost hundreds of thousands of soldiers and Germany had surely lost hope of achieving an easy victory, the war raged on. By December, German zeppelins started appearing over the British coast. In the water, German U-boats, or submarines, tried to take control over the North Sea.

One of the most important roles of the Royal Navy at this point was to defend and maintain shipping routes in the North Sea. While battles raged on the continent, British ships held the U-boats at bay so that supplies could continue to reach its allies and homeland. This preserved maritime trade between the Allied powers and its commercial partners, including the United States of America. While the Royal Navy held the sea, its land troops—including those from India—fought alongside their comrades in France.

Nevertheless, Britain was running short of military personnel, and by January of 1916, the government felt compelled to start conscripting

---

[128] "World War One Timeline." *History on the Net.* Web. 2019.

[129] Ibid.

able-bodied men for service.[130] It was not a decision that the Liberal Party took lightly, and these members of Parliament argued that to force British citizens to fight made them no better than the Kaiser, who relied on the same method. The Military Service Act, as it was called, stated that unmarried men between the ages of 18 and 41 were liable to be drafted into military service, excepting those who were widowed with children, religious leaders, or workers in necessary industries.

On May 31st, 1916, a major naval battle occurred at Jutland, a peninsula of Denmark. Hoping to break the British fleet and destroy it piece by piece, the German forces confined to the port by a British naval blockade came out fighting. British Vice-Admiral David Richard Beatty, fully aware that the Germans' naval tactics were the same as those used by Lord Nelson during the Napoleonic Wars, cleverly sent a smaller force to lure them into the range of his main fleet. The tactic proved fruitful, though the second day of fighting saw heavy losses on the British side. The Germans ultimately pulled back, however, and the seas remained under the control of the British. Later that same year, German warplanes began battering Britain for the first time, starting a terrifying and sporadic series of attacks directly on London and southeast England.

Following the bloody Battle of the Somme in France over the course of five months in the mid to latter half of 1916, British Prime Minister Lloyd George begged his government to elect a new commander in chief. No less than 420,000 British soldiers had died at the Somme, and George was horrified at the minister's attitude toward such extremely heavy losses.[131] Instead of replacing the commander in chief of the British Forces, Sir Douglas Haig, the government decided to place a new man in authority over Haig. The solution was the appointment of French General Robert Nivelle.

---

[130] "Conscription: The First World War." *Parliament*. Web.

[131] "World War One Timeline." *History on the Net*. Web. 2019.

When both of these men proved to be disappointing in their handling of the Battle of Passchendaele, which took place in Belgium in 1917, King George recruited army veteran Winston Churchill to the Cabinet to serve as the minister of munitions.

In February 1917, the British Royal Navy faced an influx of U-boats due to Germany's order that the war by sea be given a higher priority.[132] The Germans were ordered to sink both Allied and neutral vessels, and more than a million tons' worth of ships were sunk in just one month.[133] Following the upswing in violence, neutral countries were hesitant to ship goods to Britain, which forced Prime Minister Lloyd George to assign each shipment a protective convoy. Soon afterward, on April 6th, the United States of America declared war on Germany in retaliation for sinking several of its own merchant ships. In Britain, King George V officially changed his family name from Saxe-Coburg-Gotha—which was reminiscent of his German ancestry—to Windsor.

The final year of the war, 1918, began fearfully for the Allies. The Russian Revolution had taken place, and Tsar Nicolas II had been deposed. Seeking an end to the fighting after huge losses in terms of soldiers and money, the Bolsheviks in charge of the Russian interim government signed an armistice with Germany. The terms of the treaty demanded that Russia hand over Poland, Ukraine, and other occupied lands to Germany and that Russia pay 300 million rubles for the return of its prisoners of war.[134] Tsar Nicholas II and his family were assassinated later that year in July.

In Great Britain, though, the Royal Air Force had been officially formed that April, and all facets of its military fought hard with the remaining Allies. They liberated much of France and Belgium by

---

[132] Ibid.

[133] Ibid.

[134] "World War One Timeline." *History on the Net.* Web. 2019.

October with a big push called the Hundred Days Offensive, which began at the beginning of August, and accepted an armistice with the Ottoman Empire. By November 9th, Kaiser Wilhelm II abdicated his throne, and two days later, a complete armistice was signed that ended the war on the eleventh hour of the eleventh day of the eleventh month.

Chapter Twenty – The Irish Rebellions

Huge crowds gathered in London to celebrate the end of the war on November 11th, 1918. The country was jubilant and not just because the fighting was at an end. That very June, all males over the age of 21 had been granted the right to vote in elections thanks to the Representation of the People Act. Females over the age of thirty were also given the right to vote.

There were other political issues facing the country after the war, including the aftermath of Ireland's rebellion of 1916. Also known as the Easter Rising, this rebellion was an armed insurrection whose purpose was to put an end to British rule in Ireland. The insurgents wanted to create the independent Irish Republic, and they made their move while Britain was distracted by the events of the First World War. The Easter Rising lasted six days, which had been organized by a seven-man military council of the Irish Republican Brotherhood. Several Irish rebel groups, led by Patrick Pearse and James Connolly, took key positions in Dublin and proclaimed that they had taken the city for the purpose of establishing the free Irish Republic. Thousands of soldiers, as well as artillery and a gunboat, were brought in by the British Army. There were violent battles on the streets in Dublin and smaller skirmishes in rural areas, but British forces eventually defeated the Irish rebels and took back control.

On Saturday, April 29th, Pearse issued an order for all the rebels to surrender. Pearse personally offered his unconditional surrender on behalf of the Irish Republicans to British Brigadier-General William Lowe. The surrender document reads as follows:

> In order to prevent the further slaughter of Dublin citizens, and in the hope of saving the lives of our followers now surrounded and hopelessly outnumbered, the members of the Provisional Government present at headquarters have agreed to an unconditional surrender, and the commandants of the various districts in the City and County will order their commands to lay down arms.[135]

What followed was a formal British inquiry into the incident, as well as multiple arrests, trials, and executions. A total of 3,509 people was arrested, mostly members of the Sinn Féin group. British inquirers mistakenly thought that Sinn Féin, a left-wing political party formed in 1905 to put pressure on the government in favor of Irish independence, was responsible for the uprising.[136] Though nearly 200 death sentences were issued, 15 people in total were executed in legal proceedings, most of them via firing squad.[137] Those killed included Patrick Pearse and James Connolly. One woman, Constance Markievicz, was sentenced to solitary isolation, and 1,836 men were sentenced to imprisonment in English and Welsh prisons and internment camps.[138] It is likely that some of these prisoners had little or nothing to do with the rebellion in the first place.

---

[135] "Printed broadsheet announcing the unconditional surrender of the rebel forces, 30 April 1916." *National Army Museum*. Web.

[136] Cavendish, Richard. "The Foundation of Sinn Fein." *History Today*. Web.

[137] Hegarty, Shane and O'Toole, Fintan. "Easter Rising 1916." *The Irish Times*. 2016.

[138] Foy, Michael and Barton, Brian. *The Easter Rising*. 2011.

With military rule established in Ireland after the uprising, Ireland watched as its revolutionaries were dealt with en masse by the British. In the midst of such violence, even those who had been against independence started to feel differently about establishing the Irish Republic. Sentiment toward the British soured irrevocably, setting the country of Ireland even more firmly on a path to independence. The 1918 Irish general election saw a huge victory for the Sinn Féin party, and the next year, the closely related Irish Republican Army was founded.[139] On January 21st, 1919, Sinn Féin successfully pulled off a coup that left them in total control of the government, and they declared Irish independence.[140] Over the next three years, violent clashes continued between the Irish Republicans and the British Army until peace talks finally resulted in the Anglo-Irish Treaty, which went into full effect on December 6th, 1921.[141] The treaty created a political partition between northeastern Ireland and the larger portion to the south and west, where the religious and political fracture was most clear.

Over the next few years, negotiations and violence continued to wrack Ireland, and it eventually turned into a civil war between Northern and Southern Ireland. The infighting concluded with several drafts of a Constitution of the Irish Free State, the first of which was passed in 1922.[142] Later renamed the Republic of Ireland, the southern and western portions of Ireland were officially disconnected from Great Britain; the northeastern region became Northern Ireland, which still remains under British administration to this day. Northern Ireland was not only home to a majority of British

[139] O'Toole, Fintan. "The 1918 election was an amazing moment for Ireland." *The Irish Times.* 2018.

[140] "Ireland independence: Why Jan 1919 is an important date." *BBC.* Web. 21 January 2019.

[141] "Anglo-Irish Treaty – 6 December 1921." *The National Archives of Ireland.* Web.

[142] "History of Parliament in Ireland." *Houses of the Oireachtas.* Web.

loyalists but also to a majority of Anglicans. In the south, Catholics were in the majority.

The first section of the Constitution of Irelands reads as follows:

ARTICLE 1

The Irish nation hereby affirms its inalienable, indefeasible, and sovereign right to choose its own form of Government, to determine its relations with other nations, and to develop its life, political, economic and cultural, in accordance with its own genius and traditions.

ARTICLE 2

It is the entitlement and birthright of every person born in the island of Ireland, which includes its islands and seas, to be part of the Irish Nation. That is also the entitlement of all persons otherwise qualified in accordance with law to be citizens of Ireland. Furthermore, the Irish nation cherishes its special affinity with people of Irish ancestry living abroad who share its cultural identity and heritage.

ARTICLE 3

It is the firm will of the Irish Nation, in harmony and friendship, to unite all the people who share the territory of the island of Ireland, in all the diversity of their identities and traditions, recognising that a united Ireland shall be brought about only by peaceful means with the consent of a majority of the people, democratically expressed, in both jurisdictions in the island.[143]

Though it was the ultimate goal of the Irish Free State to eventually incorporate Northern Ireland into its political being, the two regions still remain at odds with one another in terms of their religious and economic futures. Anti-Irish sentiment in England was highly

---

[143] "Constitution of Ireland." *Electronic Irish Statute Book.* Web.

exacerbated for a time, but there were so many other pressing issues for its monarch and people to deal with that the discord between the two countries was mostly forgotten in time.

Chapter Twenty-One – 20th-Century England

The effects of the Irish rebellion and their fight for independence on the rest of Britain were damaging in two ways. First, the military and financial strain Britain faced while trying to outnumber and outperform organized demonstrations and political coups in Ireland was immense. Particularly given the timing during and immediately after WWI, it was difficult for the once-vast kingdom to consolidate and accept its diminishing power in the British Isles and abroad.

Politics within England were also changing, partially due to the fact that millions of Britons could vote for the first time and partly because the country faced new challenges after the turn of the century. Though it was Prime Minister Lloyd George's government that had put the new voting act into practice, his Liberal Party became deeply fragmented between supporters of Lloyd George and supporters of the previous prime minister, Herbert Henry Asquith. The divide severely weakened the Liberal Party, and it got to the point that it lost its grip on the British voting public altogether. At the same time, the post-war economy shrank as shipbuilding, coal mining, and steel manufacturing were no longer needed to support the war effort, and thousands of women who had earned salaries while men fought were forced to give up their jobs to the returning soldiers.

Strikes became commonplace as industries unionized throughout Great Britain. Even the London police force organized a massive strike in support of their union in 1918. Prime Minister Lloyd George described the situation by saying, "This country was nearer to Bolshevism that day than at any time since."[144]

1919 saw a serious miners' and railway workers' strike intended to increase workers' wages, and amid the strikes, unemployment rates rose in other sectors. The strikes began in Glasgow, Scotland, and in Belfast, Northern Ireland, at the end of January. Following the European armistice that ended World War I, engineers throughout Britain were working a 54-hour week, which, in large part, inspired the January 40 Hour Strike and its purpose in demanding a 40-hour workweek. More than 100,000 employees were led by strike committees, and during the event, there were daily public gatherings and picket lines.[145] The strike committee requested that transport trams leave the streets for the strike, but authorities refused to alter the schedules. As a result, cables from trams to overhead lines were cut down by strikers, halting the entire tram system.

If the police tried to intervene, they were chased out. Shipyard engineer Harry McShane described one incident where police tried to stop strikers from cutting the tramlines: "The strikers took off their clothes and had to run for their lives naked."[146] Despite problems with police and government officials, unions pressed forward with the strike. An estimated 2.4 million British workers went on strike throughout 1919. Most were from the railway and

---

144 Sherry, Julie. "1919 Britain in Revolt." *Socialist Worker*. Web.

145 Sherry, Julie. "1919 Britain in Revolt." *Socialist Worker*. Web.

146 Ibid.

mining sectors, both of which were primarily under government control. A special daily report issued by the Ministry of Labour on July 24th, 1919, stated that although some miners were considering going back to work, many of the coal pits were flooded and being run ineffectively by volunteers and low-ranking members of the Royal Navy.[147]

On "Bloody Friday" of 1921, a crowd of strikers was targeted by the police on the last day of January at George Square, Glasgow. Though bottles were thrown and the police used their clubs, nobody was killed. The next day, however, it quickly became clear that the government had sent in a military unit from England, along with tanks and field guns. Despite the threat, 100,000 workers went on strike again that May Day.[148]

Workers' revolts were instrumental in securing the first-ever election of Britain's Labour Party in 1924, the latter of which formed a coalition government under the leadership of Prime Minister Ramsay MacDonald. One of the major issues facing Britain's first Labour prime minister was that of debt. During the war, the country had amassed debts equal to 136 percent of its gross national product, and much of that money had come from the United States of America.[149] The United States was having an economic boom, while Britain was struggling.

Though MacDonald was forced to compromise on many of his party's policies due to his leading a coalition government, he did manage to pass the 1924 Housing Act. The Housing Act was created to alleviate the housing crisis due to a shortage of available homes. Residential building projects had dropped significantly during the war, and the Labour Party knew something had to be done so that

---

147 "Labour unrest: coal miners' strike, 1919." *The National Archives*. Web.

148 Sherry, Julie. "1919 Britain in Revolt." *Socialist Worker*. Web.

149 "Britain after the war." *The National Archives*. Web.

Britain's working class could once more find quality, affordable rental housing. Traditional Conservative governments had proposed privatization as a solution to the same problem, but MacDonald's coalition members were willing to go ahead with council housing. By 1933, this single piece of legislation had financed the development of 521,700 rental homes.[150]

Under the Labour Party's leadership, a number of welfare reforms were legislated, including access to financial benefits and unemployment insurance. Households that struggled financially now had increased government coverage for children, as well as unemployment benefits for both men and women. Payouts were increased, and the mandated length of time between one's ability to access government funds was eradicated. Retirement pensions were increased, as well as pensions for widows and war veterans. Agricultural workers had their minimum wage reinstated, worker's compensation was legislated, and schools received an impressive increase in federal grant money.

Prime Minister MacDonald was also the country's acting foreign secretary, and in the latter capacity, he focused a great deal of attention on relations between Germany, Belgium, and France. Germany had been ordered to pay reparations to the Allies but had not been able to keep up the payments. France and Belgium, in lieu of pay, moved in and occupied the most powerful economic region in Germany, the Ruhr. Thanks to a great deal of diplomatic work on the part of MacDonald and an American named Charles Dawes, France eventually agreed to give Germany time to recuperate its economy before expecting payments.

Slowly, but surely, the living conditions of the working class in Britain rose, and the industry sector found its feet. The Labour Party lost the next election but were voted in once more in 1929, just in time to watch the world's economy collapse again.

---

[150] Harmer, Harry. *The Longman Companion to The Labour Party 1900–1998*. 1999.

Chapter Twenty-Two – Edward VIII

King George V celebrated his Silver Jubilee in 1935 at the age of seventy.[151] He was a popular monarch, having gained a good reputation with the Labour Party and workers' unions during the economic depression of the 1930s. George was considered to be hardworking and loyal to his country, as well as in touch with the middle classes to a greater extent than his predecessors had been. The king's health, however, had not been the same since a fall from his horse while visiting troops in 1915. He especially suffered from pulmonary obstruction, which left him on oxygen throughout the year of the Silver Jubilee. In January of 1936, he fell unconscious in bed and stayed there for five days, intermittently coming in and out of consciousness. The royal physician administered lethal doses of morphine and cocaine to the king on January 20th, 1936; soon after, he passed away.[152]

---

[151] "George V Biography." *Biography*. Web. Updated 2019.

[152] Ibid.

Upon the king's death, the crown fell to his eldest son, Edward. Edward, Prince of Wales, was 41 years of age when he became the king of Great Britain and Northern Ireland, as well as the emperor of India.

Prince Edward VIII met Wallis Simpson, an American divorcee, in June of 1931. The two became acquainted with one another at a party hosted by Lady Thelma Furness, a mistress of Edward's, and they soon became inseparable. Having recently moved to London with her family, Wallis Simpson quickly caught the eye of the prince, who was a famous philanderer. This time, however, Prince Edward did not tire of his companion, nor did he continue to see other women while they were together. He had fallen deeply in love, but unfortunately for a member of the royal family, marrying a divorced person was simply not allowed. Furthermore, the future king of England was expected to marry a member of the European aristocracy and certainly not choose an American to be his bride.

Edward was determined, however, and he refused to break off his relationship with Simpson. Fed up with the expectations thrust onto him by the crown, King Edward made a stunning announcement via radio on December 11th, 1936.[153]

> At long last I am able to say a few words of my own. I have never wanted to withhold anything, but until now it has not been constitutionally possible for me to speak.
>
> A few hours ago I discharged my last duty as King and Emperor, and now that I have been succeeded by my brother, the Duke of York, my first words must be to declare my allegiance to him. This I do with all my heart.
>
> You all know the reasons which have impelled me to renounce the throne. But I want you to understand that in making up my mind I did not forget the country or the

---

[153] Sheddon, David. "Today in Media History: Radio stations broadcast the 1936 abdication speech of King Edward VIII." *Poynter.* 11 December 2014.

empire, which, as Prince of Wales and lately as King, I have for twenty-five years tried to serve.

But you must believe me when I tell you that I have found it impossible to carry the heavy burden of responsibility and to discharge my duties as King as I would wish to do without the help and support of the woman I love.[154]

Following the official abdication, Edward was given a new title: His Royal Highness, the Duke of Windsor. In 1937, he and Wallis Simpson were married in a private ceremony in France.[155] The newlyweds stayed in Paris for several years, simply enjoying the company of one another and their many friends. Still big news in England, the duke and his wife were often spotted in the newspapers, throwing lavish parties and spending large amounts of money shopping in the French capital.

King George VI, Edward's brother, had graciously allowed Edward to retain the "Royal Highness" part of his title, but he specifically stipulated that Wallis Simpson would not be extended the same courtesy. Though she had never been royalty, it was customary for the spouse of a royal to enjoy a cooperative title. Edward was livid at what he believed was a crass gesture, but Wallis was still allowed to use the complementary title Duchess of Windsor.

As a part of the abdication agreement, Edward received a tax-free allowance from his brother to cover his living expenses. The once-king added to this amount with money made from selling his memoirs to a publisher and by selling Balmoral Castle and Sandringham House to the new king. Neither estate was part of the royal estate, and they had been passed down to Edward privately via inheritance.

---

[154] "Edward VIII Abdicates the Throne." *The History Place*. Web.

[155] "Edward VIII." *Biography*. Web.

Eventually growing bored, Edward contacted his brother to ask whether there might be a job for him in politics. King George VI had no easy time meeting Edward's request, particularly given the fact that the Duke and Duchess of Windsor had already broken with his advice by meeting with Adolf Hitler in October of 1937.[156] The meeting was highly controversial, and rumors circulated that Edward was a personal supporter of Hitler and the Nazi regime. In defense of the Duke of Windsor, members of Edward's staff later explained that Edward had simply jumped at Hitler's invitation because he was so eager to take his wife on a state visit where she could experience the respect he believed she deserved.

Soon, even Edward and his wife had to shelter from the Nazi's regime, and while they took refuge in Lisbon, King George VI issued his brother a job as the governor of the Bahamas. It was a seemingly small position for a member of the royal family's inner circle, but to Edward and Wallis, it was a welcome invitation. For the royal family, this appointment not only kept Edward occupied, but it also kept him out of the way.

---

[156] "When the Duke of Windsor Met Adolf Hitler." *BBC News*. Web. 2016.

Chapter Twenty-Three – World War II

With King George VI still reeling from his hasty and unexpected inheritance of the throne, Europe was once more thrown into war. Again, Germany was the principal antagonist, though unlike in WWI, all of Europe had seen Adolf Hitler's rise to power and had been watching carefully, waiting for him to overstep just as Germany's previous administration had done in 1914.

Adolf Hitler had been elected chancellor of Germany in 1933, and he quickly gained a dictatorial status upon a platform of violence and fear.[157] Believing that all the people of German ancestry should be collectively ruled as one, he began annexing small territories from other countries that contained significant German populations. First, he annexed Austria; next, he made a move to occupy Czechoslovakia's Sudetenland. Citing his demands for the emancipation of the German people, Hitler quickly and boldly brought the continent to the edge of war, just as Europe was truly recovering from World War I.

---

[157] "Adolf Hitler." *Encyclopedia Britannica.* Web.

Before any fighting could break out, British Prime Minister Neville Chamberlain hurried to Germany to meet with the dictator and try to negotiate peace. In Munich, Chamberlain met with Hitler, Prime Minister Édouard Daladier of France, and Benito Mussolini of Italy. The committee all agreed that it was reasonable for the German portion of Czechoslovakia—Sudetenland—to be transferred to German rule; however, there were no diplomats or leaders from Czechoslovakia present to argue against the decision. Dangerously outnumbered, the Czechs allowed this border region to revert to Germany.

The Sudetenland was not nearly enough for Hitler, despite Chamberlain's express hopes that it would be. A mere six months after the agreement in Munich, Hitler's armies marched straight into Czechoslovakia and established military rule. In September of 1939, the German army moved into Poland, directly breaking a pact Hitler had previously made with the Soviet Union.[158] Two days later, on September 3rd, 1939, both Great Britain and France declared war on Germany.[159]

Britain took nothing for granted, having just managed to pull itself out of the depths of debt and economic crises following WWI. The government immediately reinstated military conscription and set up a secret radar warning system along its eastern coastline. The Royal Navy moved to establish a naval blockade on Germany, and gas began being rationed in order to save as much as possible for the war effort.[160]

Little movement occurred on Hitler's part until the spring of 1940; during this time, his armies attacked and took control of Norway,

---

[158] "World War Two Timeline." *History on the Net.* Web.

[159] Ibid.

[160] "What You Need to Know About Rationing in the Second World War." *Imperial War Museum.* Web. 2018.

Denmark, the Netherlands, and Belgium.[161] Immediately afterward, Neville Chamberlain resigned as the prime minister of Great Britain, and Winston Churchill was elected to be the new prime minister. Churchill's government worked quickly, recruiting factory workers and coal miners and increasing the manufacture of fighter planes.

The British government implemented food rationing in January 1940.[162] The scheme was deemed necessary to deal with food shortages brought on by the ongoing war, as the war quickly used up vast stores of resources and made it very difficult to receive more supplies from other countries. Rationing was regulated by the Ministry of Food, which outfitted each British citizen—which included men, women, and children—with a ration book filled with coupons. The coupons were required in order to buy any food items that had been put on the rationing list, and shoppers could find them at a variety of distributors. Each shopper had to register with these suppliers in order to be allowed to buy anything using the ration coupons.

The supply of coupons directly supported the purchase of kitchen staples such as sugar, meat, fats, bacon, and cheese. Other foods listed by the Ministry of Food included tinned products, dried fruit, cereal, and sweets. According to product availability and consumer demand, the distribution of such goods changed. The people judged to be the neediest, including infants and expectant mothers, were given priority selection of milk and eggs.

There were long lineups for rations, as well as many shortages. Just because a person waited in line several hours to get butter did not mean that it would be there when they reached the service desk. Fruits and vegetables were never on the rationing lists, but there were often shortages of tomatoes, onions, and imported fruits. Though meat was carefully inventoried, only the most expensive

---

[161] Ibid.

[162] Ibid.

cuts were put on the ration list. Organ meats became commonplace over cuts of muscle, leading to a wealth of new recipes and ideas for using available proteins in the most palatable way possible.

On June 4th, 1940, Prime Minister Churchill reported to the House of Commons to congratulate the country on the successful retrieval of 335,000 Allied troops from Dunkirk. He also wanted to make a clear appeal for help to the United States of America.[163]

> …The German eruption swept like a sharp scythe around the right and rear of the Armies of the north. It severed our own communications for food and ammunition, which ran first to Amiens and afterwards through Abbeville, and it shore its way up the coast to Boulogne and Calais, and almost to Dunkirk. I have said this armored scythe-stroke almost reached Dunkirk—almost but not quite.
>
> Thus it was that the port of Dunkirk was kept open. When it was found impossible for the Armies of the north to reopen their communications to Amiens with the main French Armies, only one choice remained. It seemed, indeed, forlorn. The Belgian, British and French Armies were almost surrounded. Their sole line of retreat was to a single port and to its neighboring beaches. They were pressed on every side by heavy attacks and far outnumbered in the air.
>
> When, a week ago today, I asked the House to fix this afternoon as the occasion for a statement, I feared it would be my hard lot to announce the greatest military disaster in our long history. I thought-and some good judges agreed with me-that perhaps 20,000 or 30,000 men might be re-embarked. Meanwhile, the Royal Navy, with the willing help of countless merchant seamen, strained every nerve to

---

[163] "We Shall Fight Them on the Beaches." *International Churchill Society.* Web.

embark the British and Allied troops; 220 light warships and 650 other vessels were engaged.[164]

Churchill described in vibrant detail the miraculous job that had been pulled off at Dunkirk, painting a proud picture of the British Army and their Allied comrades. He stated that he wanted every member of the House of Commons to know exactly what happened, and that is why he related the lengthy story in its entirety. When the story had been told, he went on to bolster British courage for the oncoming battles of the war and call on the United States for badly needed assistance.

> We shall go on to the end, we shall fight in France, we shall fight on the seas and oceans, we shall fight with growing confidence and growing strength in the air, we shall defend our Island, whatever the cost may be, we shall fight on the beaches, we shall fight on the landing grounds, we shall fight in the fields and in the streets, we shall fight in the hills; we shall never surrender, and even if, which I do not for a moment believe, this Island or a large part of it were subjugated and starving, then our Empire beyond the seas, armed and guarded by the British Fleet, would carry on the struggle, until, in God's good time, the New World, with all its power and might, steps forth to the rescue and the liberation of the old.[165]

The French, whose efforts had helped save theirs and British soldiers during the evacuation at Dunkirk, had nevertheless suffered intense defeats under the Germans. Defeated and with little left to contribute to the war effort, France signed an armistice on June 17th, 1940, quitting the Second World War.[166] Churchill spoke to the House of

---

[164] Ibid.

[165] Ibid.

[166] Ibid.

Commons the very next day and said, "The Battle of France is over. I expect the Battle of Britain is about to begin."[167] Britain now stood alone against Germany's military forces, which in less than two months had conquered the greater part of Western Europe. Yet Churchill pulled together his government and convinced the majority not to look toward further bargaining with Adolf Hitler, especially considering the latter's complete disregard for former alliances.

From July to October of 1940, Britain was engaged in a fierce campaign against German invaders known as the Battle of Britain.[168] Unwilling to face the Royal Navy head on, Adolf Hitler ordered his own warships to attack first, beating Britain into submission before a second wave was launched by air. This was not only the first time that Britain had sustained a powerful and direct attack, but it was the first occurrence of such a battle being fought almost entirely by aircraft. It was the Royal Air Force versus the German Luftwaffe, with the former trying desperately to keep the enemy at bay. For months, German airplanes roared overhead, dropping bombs on British air bases, military camps, and even the civilian population. Bombs rained down on London and other port cities, and mass evacuations of women and children took place so they could be in the relative safety of the countryside. The Germans also formed supply blockades, hoping to force Churchill into signing a peace treaty that was drafted by Hitler himself.

In retaliation, daring Royal Air Force pilots flew night missions, targeting Luftwaffe enemies and German ships alike, and wrenched control away from the invaders. They also flew over Berlin, returning heavy fire to the German capital, just like the Luftwaffe continued to do in London. After over three months of vicious fighting, Germany had still not managed to reduce the power of the Royal Air Force, nor take any position upon Britain's shores. Hitler

---

[167] Ibid.

[168] "Battle of Britain." *History.com.* Web. 2009.

had the Luftwaffe pull back, and the subsequent attack by sea was permanently abandoned. The decisive win of the Battle of Britain saved Great Britain from a land invasion and an eventual German occupation, also showing for the first time that air power alone was capable of winning a major battle. The bombing of London continued intermittently, though not to the horrifying extent it had been during the battle. These attacks on the capital city were collectively called the Blitz, and 60,595 British civilians were killed, and 86,182 were injured during these raids.[169]

Clothing was added to the ration list in June of 1941, and unfortunately for Great Britain, the United States of America did not formally join the war effort in Europe until after the bombing of its Pearl Harbor on December 7th, 1941. [170] [171] In February of 1942, though help was on the way, resources were scarce enough that even soap made the ration list.[172] The next two years saw the Americans flood into Great Britain to fight alongside them, and while Hitler succeeded in sending millions of prisoners he deemed unfit for his idealized Third Reich into forced labor camps and gas chambers, the Allies slowly gained a foothold on the front lines.

The German forces surrendered to the Allies in North Africa in May of 1943, but they kept fighting in Europe.[173] Japan, meanwhile, had an iron grip in the Pacific theater of the war. In 1944, the Allies concentrated on flooding France and liberating it with a steady march to Berlin. There were heavy losses on the beaches of Normandy in the first waves, but the combined American, British,

---

[169] Charman, Terry. "What life was like in Britain during the Second World War." *Imperial War Museum.* Web. 2018.

[170] "What You Need to Know About Rationing in the Second World War." *Imperial War Museum.* Web. 2018.

[171] Nelson, Craig. *From Infamy to Greatness.* 2016.

[172] Ibid.

[173] "World War II." *History of England.* Web.

and Canadian forces kept pushing, dropping tens of thousands of troops at a time until they were finally able to take some ground by the end of the summer. Paris was liberated first, followed soon afterward by Belgium and Le Havre.

Germany surrendered in May of 1945, swiftly following the suicide of Adolf Hitler as the Russian army bore down on him just fifty miles outside of Berlin.[174] The war in the Pacific continued on into the summer months until the Allies, including Winston Churchill, agreed with the Americans' plan to drop atomic bombs on Japan. The first was deployed on August 6th over Hiroshima, killing an estimated 150,000 Japanese civilians.[175] Three days later, another bomb was dropped on Nagasaki, this time killing about 75,000 people.[176] Tens of thousands more would later die due to radiation exposure.

Following the stunning devastation on the Japanese homeland, Japan formally surrendered on September 2nd, 1945.[177] Of the estimated seventy to eighty million people killed during the entire war, Britain suffered losses of about 450,900.[178] In July of 1946, Great Britain added bread to the still-growing war ration list.[179] In fact, the bulk of goods did not come off that list until the early 1950s. In 1954, food rationing finally came to an end when the last item—beef—was put back into regular circulation.[180]

---

[174] Ibid.

[175] "Hiroshima and Nagasaki Death Toll." *UCLA*. Web. 2007.

[176] Ibid.

[177] "World War II." *History of England*. Web.

[178] Ibid.

[179] "What You Need to Know About Rationing in the Second World War." *Imperial War Museum*. Web. 2018.

[180] "What You Need to Know About Rationing in the Second World War." *Imperial War Museum*. Web. 2018.

Epilogue

When the war ended, the reconstruction of London began immediately. Evacuees who had been sent to the country or the Isle of Wight for their safety returned, as did many of the troops from overseas. Workers and funds were set upon the Greater London Plan, which was a blueprint for the reconstruction of the city's docks, commercial areas, and industrial sites. The building of new homes was largely put off until the city had properly recovered, and as a result, many people were relocated—along with their jobs—to other cities. Eight new settlements outside of Greater London were founded by the New Towns Act of 1946.[181]

The British government announced the Coal Industry Nationalization Act in 1946, and the National Coal Board was established on 12 July 1946.[182] The Board was given full responsibility for managing the industry.

In 1951, the Festival of Britain was held to celebrate national recovery.

---

[181] "Reconstruction after World War II." *Encyclopedia Britannica*. Web.

[182] "Nationalisation of the Mines." *Working Class Movement Library*. Web.

Here's another book by Captivating History that we think you'd be interested in

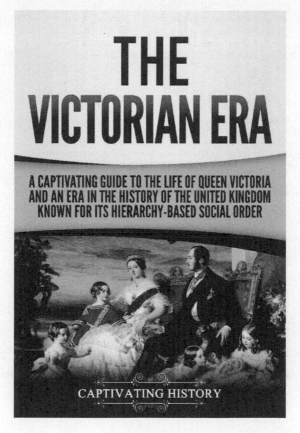

And another one…

Made in the USA
Coppell, TX
22 July 2020